Katie Stewart was cookery editor of *The Times* and is currently cookery editor of *Woman's Journal*. Among her other publications are *The Times Cookery Book* and, most recently, *The Katie Stewart Cook Book*. She lives in Cuckfield, Sussex where her spare time is occupied mainly by gardening.

Pamela Michael was researcher and compiler for two of Katie Stewart's previous books, *Food for Lovers* and *Cooking and Eating*, before writing *All Good Things Around Us*. She enjoys writing and cooking in equal measure and lives and works near Lostwithiel, Cornwall.

WILD BLACKBERRY COBBLER
AND OTHER OLD FASHIONED RECIPES

KATIE STEWART & PAMELA MICHAEL

Futura

A Futura Book
Copyright © Grub Street, London, 1984

First published in Great Britain in 1984 by
J.M. Dent & Sons Ltd, London

This edition published in 1985 by
Futura Publications, a Division of
Macdonald & Co (Publishers) Ltd
London & Sydney

ISBN 0 7088 2864 7

Printed in Great Britain by
The Guernsey Press

Futura Publications
A Division of
Macdonald & Co (Publishers) Ltd
Maxwell House
74 Worship Street
London EC2A 2EN
A BPCC plc Company

CONTENTS

INTRODUCTION TO THE RECIPES

There is a growing revolt against man-made materials and processed food. It is a quiet revolution in which people are discovering the value of more natural things, and in which old customs and handcrafts are being revived and a new interest is being taken in the eating habits and food of earlier generations.

The recipes in this book are all old ones. They illustrate the variety and quality of the food our forebears enjoyed. They never knew such things as tinned and packaged food, nor supermarkets where such foods are sold. There were no eggs from battery hens, no factory-farmed meat, no ultra-heat-treated milk. Chemical farming, monoculture and microwaves were as remote to them as the moon then was, but is no longer. Their food was produced naturally and according to the seasons; their stoves cooked gently and their cooks were artists in the blending of flavours. No wonder that we should reach back to their more wholesome way of life.

One of the fascinating aspects of the recipes in this book is a chain that links much of the food throughout the ages. One can find links in Roman cooking with that of the Middle Ages in the ingredients common to both such as saffron, cinnamon, ginger and almonds, olive oil and wine, as well as most of the herbs, many of which were introduced into the rest of Europe by the Romans.

The early Persian and Indian food which has remained virtually unchanged for centuries contains these same flavourings which must be ancient indeed. Cloves, saffron, cinnamon, ginger, cumin and coriander occur throughout them all, with pepper, which is still an everyday seasoning in every modern household. These spices reached Greece and Rome through the Middle East from the famous Spice Islands of the East Indies, and lingered in diminished use in Europe until the revival of trade and the Crusaders brought them back to popularity in the Middle Ages. Some of the ingredients that were freely used in classical and medieval times would be considered extravagant today: saffron was widely grown even in England, and our precious olive oil was of so little account in ancient Greece that when a cook wanted more heat quickly, he would fling some olive oil onto the fire.

Despite the close link between Greek and Roman food, the two were very different in character and though many of the ingredients were common to both, they prepared them in quite dissimilar ways. The Greeks liked their food plain and simple and, according to Athenaeus, the Greek writer on table manners, conversation and food, the true gourmet despised elaborate sauces and too many spices. However, the fact that Athenaeus scorned them suggests that some people must have indulged in them.

But the Romans, though many of their cooks, carvers and servants were Greek, delighted in food that combined many flavours. Roman food, as handed down to us in the rare descriptions and recipes that survive had a highly original and very clear, refreshingly aromatic flavour that was sharp and piquant, never cloying or heavy. Puddings as such were almost unknown. One or two references to an egg custard and an earlier Greek cheese cake are nearly all that are mentioned in the writings of the Roman epicure Apicius and the works of Athenaeus. Figs, eaten on their own or with bread are often mentioned, and presumably fresh fruit was more to their taste than cooked desserts.

The Roman satirist, Juvenal, gave several descriptions of food and eating habits. In one, he castigated the *nouveaux riches* for giving elaborate banquets for their friends and lavishing upon them lobsters, asparagus and peacocks, while their clients – poor gentlemen and writers like Juvenal – were served with polluted Tiber eel and stale olive oil. He ridiculed Apicius who paid a small fortune for one exceptionally large red mullet while people like himself were living in attics and tenement blocks, unable to light a fire to cook their meals for fear of burning the whole building down. Juvenal's idea of perfect food was good, wholesome country fare and in of the later satires, when his fortunes had improved, he invited a friend to dinner at his home and warned him that he need expect no extravagant delicacies, but would be served with food from Juvenal's own farm: chicken, young lamb, new-laid eggs, fresh fruit and herbs picked on the hills by the shepherd's wife. As in all affluent societies, there were eccentrics who craved the simpler life in the midst of opulence. The nineteenth century German scientist Rumohr who was an advocate of simple, natural foods and our modern health food movement are close parallels of Juvenal's disgust with an over-elaborate urban way of life.

The instructions in the old books of cookery are delightfully vague, and very individual. The Roman instructions seem terse, even peremptory: 'Pound pepper, rue, onion, savoury, a little wine, garum and oil'; 'chop hard-boiled eggs, add pepper, cumin, parsley, honey – not too much – boiled leek, some myrtle berries'. The medieval books instruct one 'to take' this or that 'and seeth hem wel in gode broth, wyne greke and a porcian of vynegar . . .and when 'tis done serve it forth'. Sometimes we are even told to 'messe it forth'. Nowadays, we are so used to precise instructions for weights and measures, methods and oven temperatures that at first it seems confusingly vague to 'Strew on enow gode powdour', or 'to do it wel', but, after all, cooking is always a matter of good judgement and individual taste. The cooks of the Middle Ages gave us all the necessary ingredients, a guide to the method, and left us with the inspiration to create a good dish.

Occasionally the instructions were amazingly exact as with the famous recipe for 'Lamprays Bake', which contains a detailed description of how to kill and bleed the lampreys, how to cut, clean, scald, marinate and season them before curling them round in 'cofyns of fyne paste' (a pastry case) 'then keyvere hym fayre with a lede, ave a lytel hole in the mydelle, and at the hool, blow in the cofynne with thin mouthe a gode blast of wynde. And soddenly stoppe the hole, that the wynd a-byde with ynne, to reyse uppe the cofynne, that he fall nowt-a-downne'. We were tempted to try this ingenious trick of 'a gode blast of wynde', but felt we had better stick to baking powder, fats and eggs as our raising agents for pastry!

In the medieval recipes that exist there are more desserts than in the Roman ones, though we have the impression that fruit was eaten in preference to cooked dishes whenever fresh fruit was in season. Their puddings were made with dried fruits such as dates, figs and raisins, as well as apples and pears which store well, so cooked desserts were probably mostly eaten in the winter and spring. Many of the recipes using dried fruit were laced with wine and ginger, cinnamon and cloves and when being cooked on a wintry day send wafts of a most delicious warm and spicy aroma about the house. The old books give many appetizing ways of cooking meat, fish, poultry and vegetables, as well as game. The people of the Middle Ages considered porpoises were fish and several recipes for the preparation and cooking of porpoise exist as well as many ways of cooking and serving lake and river fish such as roach, tench, perch and lampreys. The water must have beautifully clear and unpolluted compared with most lakes and rivers today, as anyone who has tried the muddy flavour of roach or tench will agree.

A lot of historical nonsense has been talked about medieval food, most of it based on the assumption that spicy flavourings were needed to disguise the taste of tainted meat. This theory ignores the fact that the countryside teemed with wild life; for there was game for those who could hunt or poach it, and fresh fish and small birds which the ordinary people caught with nets and slings and snares, a wretched practice which still survives in southern Europe today. Farm animals were kept for meat, although few were overwintered because the ways of drying and storing fodder crops were limited. However, country people cultivated vegetables, even townspeople had gardens and, because towns were small, were able to buy country produce in shops and markets. Many edible common weeds and wild plants were used in cooking as well as for medicine, so the medieval folk were not entirely dependent on agriculture for freshness and variety in their diet. They had the same natural incentive common to all cooks, to prepare food that tastes good and looks appetizing, they loved the flavour of spices and were concerned with the appearance of their food. Saffron was often mentioned purely as a colouring agent, and they used 'saunders' for the rich red colouring made from sandalwood. Dishes were 'endored' (gilded) with saffron and egg yolks, and 'flourished' with powdered spices, herbs and even sugar, which was then vastly expensive. Medieval food should not be disparaged, but judged instead by the many delicious recipes available to us.

Forks were used for carving but not for eating with until the late sixteenth century, which accounts for the instructions for much of the medieval food to be 'hacked', or chopped, small. By the seventeenth century the fork was firmly established and the medieval style of cooking had virtually disappeared, but the fork was not the only factor that brought a change in fashion to the gourmets of western Europe. Sugar became more plentiful, and therefore cheaper, and interesting new ingredients were being introduced from the Far East and the Americas. Before the discovery of America, the only beans grown and eaten in Europe were broad beans, but varieties of the now-familiar kinds of smooth-podded green beans were being introduced to Europe. From the New World, too, came the first large-fruited strawberries, *Fragaria virginiana* and *F. chiloensis*, the luscious forebears of our garden strawberries. Before that the little wild strawberry was all that was known in Europe and though gardeners had tried to develop strains with large fruits from wild plants ('big Berries as Berries of the Bramble in the hedge' were described), a strawberry as big as a blackberry would still fall far short of the large garden strawberry of today. A wider variety of vegetables was now being grown and more members of the cabbage family, such as cauliflower and broccoli, are mentioned in the recipes. Food began to change its character; gone are the long lists of spices and herbs and the multiplicity of ingredients, instead we find perhaps two or three flavourings which complement or contrast with each other. Cooks no longer wanted to alter the original taste of the food, but rather to enhance it with complementary flavours. One cannot be sure of the reason for this: food obviously reflects, to a certain extent, the character of the society which eats it, but it is perhaps too facile to say that the rich, late medieval food reflected the love of extravagance, the sumptuousness of dress and the intricacy of architecture, while the seventeenth century's more subtle style of cooking reflected the return to classical simplicity of, for example, Palladian architecture and the classical forms of literature. Whatever the reason, the new Italian style of cooking was spreading north and west and laying the foundations for the *haute cuisine* of the nineteenth century.

Eighteenth- and nineteenth-century Britain produced the golden age of cheap, efficient labour and lavish abundance in the kitchen. Huge amounts of butter, cream and eggs were used and, in the recipes that follow, have had to be reduced in quantity for smaller modern families and more modest tastes. Legs of veal, pounds of ham and several chickens might be used simply for a stock with which to enrich a sauce. Almonds were still freely used, as in all European and Middle Eastern cookery from Roman times onwards. It is obvious, from the recipes, that nothing was too much trouble, and the most gloriously rich ingredients were not considered extravagant. In many of the eighteenth-century English cookery books there are sometimes disparaging references to French cooking, though whether dictated by politics or taste is not clear, and there are frequent patronising comments on the simplicity and thick-headedness of servants in general.

Many of the recipes had comments of a medical nature such as 'this dish cannot be said to contain either gout or scurvy' or 'this is a very wholesome soup for all ages and constitutions, and will be very proper for those who the day before have plentifully eat of a fiery turtle soup'. When wholesome soups could no longer assuage the pangs of indigestion, a trip to Bath or Tunbridge Wells might be necessary. There the sufferer would not only 'take the waters', and unaccustomed exercise, but would also be provided with plainer food. At Tunbridge Wells, a special delicacy was wheatear pie. These little ground-nesting birds were all too easily trapped on the South Downs and brought in quantity to the Wells every day, where they were eagerly devoured by ailing gourmands whose jaded appetites played a drastic part in the reduction in numbers of the once common wheatears.

The desserts, at this time, were perfumed with ambergris or strewn with tiny sweetmeats. Some recipes bear delightfully fulsome titles such as 'The Best

INTRODUCTION

Orange Pudding That Ever Was Tasted', 'To Make Westphalia-Hams; absolutely the best way to do them', or 'this was given by one of the nicest House-wives in England; and is as good as ever was made'. It was an age of such confidence and such abundance!

There are recipes for heron, swan, curlew, lapwing and every sort of game; the countryside still supported an abundance of wild life. Housewives tackled recipes for the captains of ships: 'To make a catchup that will keep twenty years. You may carry it to the Indies'. They loved to disguise dishes, and gave ways of serving venison that was not venison: 'If you use mutton over 5 years old no one will discover the deception'; or 'to dress halibut in the manner of Scotch collops during Lent'. There are many recipes for use in illness, and they were not afraid to tackle cures for the most dangerous maladies. Along with descriptions of delicious foods are remedies such as 'a certain cure for the bite of a mad dog'; 'receipt against the plague'; or a recipe for 'hysterical water' containing so many poisons such as 'mistletoe of the oak' that though sensibly diluted, the drink would have had a dramatically stupefying effect. There is advice on 'how to keep clear from bugs' and 'how to wash silver lace that is tarnished' as well as how to prevent 'the infection among horned cattle'. Every country household was self-sufficient and the housewife had to be cook, brewer, baker, pharmacist and vet. The wonder is she had time left to invent so many delectable dishes.

However, the resourcefulness of the eighteenth- or nineteenth-century housewife was small compared with that of the early American settlers' wives. They not only had to turn their hands to any and everything, but had to be prepared to start with a life of camping, then adapt themselves to a settled farm and finally, if they were lucky, perhaps to become the grand lady of a large household. They had to cope with a bewildering array of new ingredients in their new land: one of the most important was Indian corn, or maize, and another the green, red and yellow peppers and chillies of the Mexican Indians which so influenced the cooking of the southwestern United States.

The Creole and French influence is very noticeable in the recipes from the southern states, and has provided a most happy blend of traditional dishes. Pennsylvania produced a special type of German cooking brought by the early settlers who came to be known as the Pennsylvania 'Dutch', a corruption of the word *Deutsch*. They were rightly famous for their home-baking, and for wholesome, nourishing dishes. There is an appetizing, homespun quality about most of the early American recipes, New England and the South providing the more sophisticated cooking. The Americans have some delicious berries, as well as some fabulous fish and shellfish, particularly off the west coast. Abalone, black bass, cioppine, clam and tuna, as well as a prolific supply of crab, lobster and Pacific salmon, provide a richness and variety of seafood that Europeans do not enjoy.

The early Australian settlers had an even harsher climate and land to wrestle with and what to them must have seemed even stranger new animals and plants to incorporate into their diet. Once the sheep and cattle ranchers were established and the wonderful fruit-growing areas under cultivation, the new

INTRODUCTION

Australians had a wealth of top quality ingredients for their menus, as well as a whole new range of seafood.

The delights of many of these sea creatures are forbidden to the Muslims of Persia and India and those fish which they allowed to eat must have been impossible to obtain except for people who lived on the coast. The cooking of Persia and India relies almost exclusively on meat and vegetables for the main dishes, with rice. As would be expected, they are full of aromatic spices and the flavourings tend to be subtle, with a blend of three or four spices for each dish, rather than too many conflicting flavours which the rather harsh-tasting commercial curry-powders seem to contain. Middle Eastern desserts have not changed for centuries, and are what we would describe as sweetmeats rather than puddings. Sweet loaves, dipped in syrup scented with rosewater or orange flower water and rolled in scented sugar, are found in El Baghdadi's thirteenth-century manual of cooking, and these and many other traditional dishes can be found in modern books of Middle Eastern cookery today.

The Chinese recipes in this book range from a sixth-century dish that was a favourite of one of the royal concubines of the Tang dynasty, to a more sophisticated recipe of stir-fried chicken and shrimp of the eighteenth century. Chinese cooking is still strongly traditional and uses many of the same ingredients and methods that were in use in the days of the ancient spice trade when China was one of the main exporters of spices to Europe and the Middle East.

These recipes are all supplied by Kenneth Lo, the famous cookery writer and owner of a gourmet Chinese restaurant in London and therefore retain his individuality. He began his career in the 1930s as a diplomat and became interested in cookery when some early handbooks on household management and cooking turned up in the family's library.

Some readers may wonder why there are no veal dishes in the recipes, since many of the old books included recipes for veal. The omission is intentional. Apart from the horrifying conditions under which veal is produced today which prompt many people to avoid it as a matter of principle, modern veal bears no resemblance to that of the past. The almost tasteless, dry white meat from artificially fed calves is quite unlike the succulent flesh obtained from the slowly-reared young animals that fed on fresh milk and natural fodder in the days preceding factory farming, and the old recipes would be impossible to reproduce using veal produced under modern conditions.

MEASURES

Where teaspoons appear in a recipe it is assumed that they are rounded. Where a mean or generous measure is called for the directions read 'level' or 'heaped' tea- or tablespoons.

AUTHOR'S NOTE

Modern recipes for short crust, puff and flaky pastry have been included in the book only for the sake of convenience to the reader.

GREEK AND ROMAN RECIPES FROM CLASSICAL TIMES

In order to follow the recipes faithfully you should have a small supply of coriander, cumin and caraway seeds and pine kernels which are all available from health food shops, and, as well as thyme, oregano, parsley and mint, a few of the more unusual herbs such as lovage, rue and savory. These can all be easily grown in the garden, or bought dried from branches of Culpeper or fresh from good greengrocers and specialist herb growers. The Greeks and Romans had no sugar and never cooked with butter, so honey was used for sweetening and lots of olive oil and wine went into their dishes.

Passum was specially sweetened wine. Where this is called for in a recipe, sweet white wine in which a few raisins have been soaked or with a little honey added is a good substitute.

Defrutum was prepared from must and new wine and a substitute can be achieved by pressing the juice from some grapes and boiling it up to reduce a little. It adds a subtle flavour to a dish.

Finally, no Roman recipe is complete without **garum** or **liquamen** (the words are interchangeable) which was the seasoning they used instead of salt. In the *Geoponica*, an early collection of Greek and Roman writings on practical agriculture and husbandry, the author describes how factory-made **garum** was produced involving a lengthy process of drying fish in the sun. Luckily it also mentions a quick method for small households, which explains how to make brine and test its strength by floating an egg in it, then boiling fish such as sprats, mullet, mackerel or anchovies in the brine until it began to reduce. Flavourings of oregano and defrutum were sometimes added, then the liquid was cooled, strained two or three times until it was clear, then sealed and stored away. If you cannot be bothered to make the experiment, then use salt for seasoning to suit your taste, but the salty liquid garum distributes its taste very evenly and harmoniously and can be used in any dish requiring salt, not just a Roman dish. Here is a simple way of making it which will keep for weeks.

Defrutum

¾lb/340 g red or white grapes

Press the grapes through a sieve or food mill into a small saucepan. Bring the juice slowly to boiling point and allow to boil gently for a few minutes until the juice has reduced a little. Cool and use straight away.

Garum

½ lb (225 g) salt
1½ pints (850 ml) water
6 tinned anchovy fillets

1 level teaspoon (5 ml) oregano
6 tablespoons (90 ml) defrutum
(optional)

Stir the salt into the water until it dissolves. Pour into a saucepan and add the anchovies, oregano and defrutum, or grape juice, if used. Bring to the boil, and cook briskly for 15 minutes. Cool, strain through muslin three or four times until the liquid is free of bits and fairly clear. When cold, bottle, or keep in a screw-topped jar.

About 2-3 teaspoons (10-15 ml) of garum are equal in strength to ¼ teaspoon (1.25 ml) salt for seasoning.

IN OVIS HEPALIS
SOFT-BOILED EGGS WITH PINE KERNEL SAUCE

This delicious and unusual dish makes the perfect starter for a lunch party. Pine kernels and lovage are really necessary in the recipe for the very subtle flavour they give to the sauce. Lovage tastes strongly of celery, which can be used as a substitute if you cannot buy fresh lovage or do not grow it in the garden. It is a tall, robust herb which grows like a weed, and the leaves and stems are the parts used.

These eggs, which are soft-boiled and eaten cold, are served in France today as *oeufs mollets*. They are particularly good in this Roman version with the sharp-sweet sauce, which has the consistency of mayonnaise, spooned over the eggs just before serving.

Serves 4

4 eggs
3 oz (85 g) pine kernels, soaked
overnight
1 tablespoon (15 ml) finely chopped
lovage leaves, or chopped celery
stems and leaves

½ teaspoon (2.5 ml) honey
1½ tablespoons white wine vinegar
1 teaspoon garum (page 13)
freshly milled black pepper

Lower the eggs gently into boiling water and simmer for 5 minutes. Plunge into cold water and leave for 8 minutes. Carefully peel away the shells and keep the eggs submerged in cold water until ready for use. Put the pine kernels into an electric liquidizer (the Romans used slaves and a pestle and mortar) and blend to a creamy consistency. Pour into a bowl and stir in the finely chopped lovage leaves or celery stems and leaves, the honey and wine vinegar. Add the garum and plenty of freshly milled black pepper. Stir until thoroughly mixed.

Arrange the eggs in a shallow dish with the sauce spooned over. Serve with thin slices of brown bread and butter.

Patina Solearum
SOLE POACHED IN WINE WITH A HERB SAUCE

The sauce, in which either fillets or small whole fish are cooked, has a taste of vinaigrette and fresh greenery. It is a most delicate complement to the naturally good flavour of fresh sole. The Romans had a rich variety of sauces, so they must have eaten with spoons as much as with their fingers. Wine was used freely in their sauces, which, as one writer described, should have 'a seductive feel that caressed the mouth'.

Serves 4

4 small Dover sole or about 1½ lb (680 g) filleted sole
3 tablespoons (45 ml) olive oil
2 teaspoons (10 ml) garum (page 13)
½ pint (284 ml) dry white wine
2 tablespoons (30 ml) fresh lovage leaves, chopped, or chopped celery stems and leaves

2 teaspoons (10 ml) fresh or ½ teaspoon (2.5 ml) dried oregano
freshly milled black pepper
1 large or 2 small eggs

Clean and skin the soles if whole fish are used. Place the fish in a shallow saucepan with the oil, garum and wine. Cover and poach gently for 10-15 minutes until the fish is cooked, then remove from the heat.

Put the lovage, oregano and pepper into a bowl with 3 tablespoons (45 ml) of the liquid in which the fish has cooked. Stir in the lightly mixed egg. Slowly pour this mixture over the fish in the pan. Return the pan to a low heat and heat slowly, stirring occasionally to keep the sauce smooth. Lift the fish onto a hot serving dish and spoon over the sauce. Sprinkle with a little freshly milled pepper and serve hot.

AD AVES OMNI GENERE
CHICKEN BAKED IN A PASTRY CASE

Nothing could be more succulent than this method of cooking a chicken wrapped in a flour and oil paste. All the juices and flavour of the chicken are retained. For the sake of economy, sunflower or even maize oil could be used instead of olive oil, but the Greeks and Romans, with their beautifully tended olive-groves and Mediterranean climate, had no need for substitutes and used nothing but olive oil in their cooking.

Serves 4

1 fresh chicken, about 3½ lb (1¾ kg)
a little olive oil

For the paste
1½ lb (680 g) plain flour
½-¾ pint (284-420 ml) olive oil

Wipe the chicken and then brush it all over with oil. Set aside while preparing the flour and oil paste.

Sift the flour into a bowl and stir in enough oil, mixing well, to make a soft dough. Turn out on to a floured working surface and divide the dough into two unequal parts. Press the smaller piece out with the hands until it is slightly larger than the chicken all round. Lay the chicken in the centre. Press out the larger piece and drape it over the bird. Press the edges well together to completely seal the chicken inside the paste. Lightly oil a roasting tin and place the paste-wrapped chicken on it. Bake in the centre of a moderately hot oven (190°C, 375°F, Gas 5) for 2¼ hours. The addition of a paste jacket considerably increases the baking time.

When the cooking time is complete, break open the crust and lift out the chicken. Serve with the sauce featured in the next recipe.

IUS CANDIDUM IN AVEM ELIXAM
PIQUANT SAUCE TO SERVE WITH POULTRY

This white sauce should be used sparingly, as you would mustard, or mint sauce. It is good hot or cold. Almonds, hazel nuts or walnuts can be used, or a mixture of all three. At a Roman meal this sauce would have been served with a capon or goose for the main course. Each course was set on a table which was carried in when needed and inserted into a U-shaped arrangement of couches on which the diners reclined. When they had finished a course the table was withdrawn and another with the next course ready laid on it, inserted in its place.

Serves 4

2 oz (55 g) blanched almonds
½ level teaspoon (2.5 ml) ground pepper
1 tablespoon (15 ml) finely chopped lovage leaves, or celery stems and leaves
1 level teaspoon (5 ml) ground cumin
1 level teaspoon (5 ml) celery seed

2 teaspoons (10 ml) garum (page 13)
1 teaspoon (5 ml) honey
2 tablespoons (30 ml) olive oil
3 tablespoon (45 ml) white wine vinegar

Lightly toast the almonds and grind them coarsely into a bowl. Add the pepper, lovage, cumin, celery seed, garum and honey. Stir in the oil and vinegar. At this stage the mixture should be fairly runny as the nuts will absorb the liquid. Pour into a small saucepan and simmer very gently for 10 minutes. Remove from the heat and allow to stand in a warm place for 30 minutes.

Reheat gently just before serving.

Haedum Sive Agnum Parthicum
ROAST LAMB WITH SPICY PLUM SAUCE

Kid can be difficult to obtain, but lamb is a perfectly good alternative. The sauce which accompanies this dish of roast lamb tastes spicy sweet, rather like a good mild chutney. The original recipe used damsons which, if obtainable, would be simply delicious as would any cooking plum. When fresh fruit is not obtainable, use prunes first simmered in a little red wine until they are tender. Rue is a pungent herb and not easy to come by unless you grow it in the garden. Although it tastes quite unlike sage, you could substitute sage as it is also pungent and the quantity needed is very small. The Romans loved a mixture of herbs and fruit to be used in sauces with meat much as we use apple sauce and cranberry sauce and mint and parsley.

Serves 6

shoulder of lamb, about 4 lb (1¾ kg) in weight
oil for roasting

For the sauce
10 cooking plums or 10 cooked prunes
2 onions
3 tablespoons (45 ml) olive oil
½ teaspoon (2.5 ml) ground pepper
1 teaspoon (5 ml) finely chopped rue or sage leaves
3 teaspoons (15 ml) fresh marjoram or 1 teaspoon (5 ml) dried
3 teaspoons (15 ml) garum (page 13)
½ pint (284 ml) red wine
1 tablespoon (15 ml) white wine vinegar

Roast the lamb with a little oil in the roasting tin in a hot oven (200°C, 400°F, Gas 6) for 1¾ hours or until nicely brown and crisp on the outside.

Meanwhile, prepare the sauce. Stone the plums or prunes and chop roughly. Peel and chop the onions. Heat the oil in a saucepan, add the onions and fry gently until soft. Add the pepper, rue, marjoram, garum, plums or prunes and wine. Cook gently for about 15 minutes. Just before serving add the vinegar.

Hand the sauce separately in a sauce-boat, or carve the meat on to a hot dish and spoon the sauce over.

HAEDEM SIVE AGNNAMEX CALDATUM
HOT KID OR LAMB STEW

A reasonably cheap cut such as middle neck of lamb is ideal for this tender stew, fragrant with herbs and wine, which conjure up the delights of the Roman countryside. It is simple to prepare and can be kept hot without spoiling.

Serves 4

3 lb (1½ kg) middle neck of lamb
1 large onion
1 tablespoon (15 ml) ground coriander
freshly milled black pepper
½ teaspoon (2.5 ml) ground cumin
2 tablespoons (30 ml) chopped lovage leaves, or celery stems and leaves

½ pint (284 ml) dry white wine
3 tablespoons (45 ml) olive oil
3 teaspoons (15 ml) garum (page 13)
1 rounded teaspoon (1.25 ml) cornflour

Trim surplus fat from the lamb and cut into neat pieces. Peel and finely slice the onion. Put the lamb pieces and onion into a saucepan, add the coriander, a seasoning of pepper, the cumin and lovage. Pour in the white wine, olive oil and garum. Bring slowly to the boil, then cover and simmer gently for 1½ hours.

Lift out the lamb pieces and keep warm. Strain the gravy into a saucepan and reserve the herbs and onion pieces retained in the strainer. Blend the cornflour with a little cold water, add a small amount of the gravy, mix well and pour back into the saucepan with the rest of the gravy. Bring up to the boil, stirring until the mixture has thickened. Add the onion and herbs from the strainer, reheat, then pour over the meat and serve.

PORCELLUM AENOCOCTUM
PORK ROASTED WITH AROMATIC HERBS AND SPICES

This method of roasting pork is so delicious that if you cook no other Roman recipe we recommend you try this one. Pork roasted any other way will afterwards seem dull in comparison. The original recipe is for sucking-pig, but a good loin of pork cooks into an aromatic and succulent dish. The recipe tells us to cook the pig in a metal pan; the Roman *batterie de cuisine* was quite impressive, they had bronze frying-pans, cauldrons, scoops, ladles, strainers, colanders, fish-kettles and cake pans. For this recipe a self-basting roasting tin is ideal.

Serves 6

3 tablespoons (45 ml) olive oil
1 loin of pork with the rind on, about
4½ lb (2 kg)
½ pint (284 ml) red wine
¼ pint (142 ml) water
4 teaspoons (20 ml) garum (page 13)
2 tablespoons (30 ml) ground coriander
1 leek, washed and sliced in half
lengthwise
6 tablespoons (90 ml) defrutum
(page 13)

For the sauce
½ teaspoon (2.5 ml) ground pepper
1 tablespoon (15 ml) chopped lovage
leaves, or celery stems and leaves
1 teaspoon (5 ml) crushed caraway seeds
½ teaspoon (2.5 ml) celery seed
1 teaspoon (5 ml) dried oregano
3 tablespoons (45 ml) passum (page 12)
3 tablespoons (45 ml) red wine
1 level tablespoon (15 ml) cornflour

Heat the oil in a metal casserole or self-basting roasting tin over direct heat. Add the pork and brown gently on all sides, then add the red wine, the water and half the garum with the coriander and the leek. Cover, place in a hot oven (200°C, 400°F, Gas 6) and roast, allowing 25 minutes per pound (450 g) and 25 minutes extra. Halfway through the cooking time, pour the defrutum over the pork and lower the temperature to moderately hot (190°C, 375°F, Gas 5) if the pork is browning too fast.

Place the pepper, lovage, caraway, celery seed and oregano in a saucepan. Add the rest of the garum, the passum, the red wine and 3 tablespoons (45 ml) of the liquid in which the pork is cooking. Bring to the boil and simmer together for 15 minutes. Draw off the heat and set aside.

Dish up the pork and pour off some of the fat remaining in the roasting tin. Blend the cornflour with a little cold water and then stir into the mixture in the saucepan. Pour the contents of the pan into the juices in the roasting tin. Bring to the boil, stirring all the time until the sauce thickens. Serve separately in a sauce-boat with a grinding of black pepper added.

PORROS

This unusual recipe for leeks can be served hot or cold. As a starter, or part of an *hors d'oeuvre* they are best cold, but as a hot vegetable, return the dressed leeks and butter beans to the pan and heat them through together before serving. The variety of ways in which salads and vegetables were served shows how imaginative and skilled the cooks were. In Roman times, the cooks were usually Greek, and they obviously had a great feeling for vegetables, dating back to their less elaborate culture.

Serves 4

6 oz (170 g) dried butter beans, soaked overnight
1½ lbs (¾ kg) leeks
3 tablespoons (45 ml) olive oil

2 teaspoons (10 ml) garum (page 13)
2½ tablespoons (37.25 ml) dry white wine

Drain the soaked butter beans and place in a saucepan. Cover with fresh cold water, bring up to the boil and simmer for 45 minutes or until tender. Then drain well.

Trim and wash the leeks. Cook in boiling water for 10-15 minutes or until tender. Drain well and place in a serving dish. Dress with olive oil, garum and the wine. Stir in the butter beans.

MINUTAL EX PRAECOQUIS
FRICASSEE OF PORK WITH SPICED SWEET-SOUR SAUCE

In this recipe a piece of pork is first roasted then diced and cooked with apricots, spices and wine until it is reduced to a tender, fricassee-like consistency. The Romans sometimes used crumbled pastry to thicken their sauces and gravies. It works perfectly well and leaves no unusual taste, but one could use a crumbled Weetabix, plain crushed biscuit or even a little coarse wholemeal flour without noticeably altering the dish, which is full of the flavour of spices and herbs.

Serves 4-6

1 piece leg of pork, about 3½ lb (1½ kg)
3 shallots or 1 small onion
4 tablespoons (60 ml) olive oil
½ pint (284 ml) dry white wine
4 teaspoons (20 ml) garum (page 13)
¼ lb (115 g) fresh apricots or dried apricots, soaked overnight
¼ level teaspoon (1.25 ml) ground black pepper

1 teaspoon (5 ml) ground cumin
1 teaspoon (5 ml) dried mint
3 teaspoons (15 ml) dried dill weed
3 teaspoons (15 ml) honey
2 tablespoons (30 ml) white wine vinegar
1 tablespoon (15 ml) passum (page 13)
a piece of pastry or a plain biscuit

Put the pork in an oiled roasting tin, place in a moderately hot oven (180°C, 375°F, Gas 5) and roast allowing 25 minutes per pound (450 g) and 25 minutes extra. Remove from the tin, cut the roasted pork into dice and place in a saucepan. Peel and chop the shallots and add to the pork along with the oil, wine and 4 teaspoons (20 ml) of the garum. Cook gently for 30 minutes. Halve and stone the fresh apricots. If using dried apricots, simmer the soaked fruit in a little water for 30 minutes or until tender, then drain.

Put the black pepper, cumin, mint, dill, honey, remaining 2 teaspoons (10 ml) of garum, vinegar and sweet white wine into a bowl. Add ¼ pint (142 ml) of the cooking liquor from the pork. Mix well and return to the saucepan in which the pork is cooking. Add the apricots, cover and continue to simmer gently for a further hour until all the ingredients are very tender. About 5 minutes before serving, stir in some crumbled pastry (about the size of a small saucer), a Weetabix or a plain biscuit. Stir gently to thicken the gravy and serve.

Perna
HAM WITH FIGS

When ham or gammon is boiled with dried figs it acquires a wonderful flavour. If you want to follow this recipe exactly you should finish cooking the ham in a paste covering made from flour and olive oil which keeps the flesh beautifully moist. Using olive oil is expensive (since you do not eat the crust) and you can still achieve a fine honey-baked ham by simply glazing the joint in the oven. Any left over is delicious cold.

Serves 6-8

4 lb (1¾ kg) gammon, soaked in cold   *Flour and oil paste (page 16)*
water for several hours
½ lb (225 g) dried figs
3 bay leaves
2 tablespoons (30 ml) honey

Drain the soaked gammon and rinse well. Place in a large saucepan with the figs and bay leaves and add fresh cold water to cover. Bring to the boil, cover and simmer for 1½ hours.

Lift the gammon from the pan, drain well and allow to cool for a few moments. Using a sharp knife, carefully remove the rind. Make criss-cross incisions in the fat and spread the honey over the surface so the cuts are filled.

Roll out the flour and oil paste, place the gammon in the centre and wrap the dough around it, pressing the edges together well to seal the gammon inside. Place on an oiled baking tray. Set in a moderately hot oven (190°C, 175°F, Gas 5) and bake for 45 minutes. Break the crust open to remove the gammon and serve hot.

Note: If you want to omit the paste, about 30 minutes in a moderately hot oven will be enough to bake the ham and brown the surface.

GASTRIS – according to Chrysippus
NUT CAKES WITH HONEY

This recipe comes from *The Deipnosophistai*, or Sophists at Dinner, by the famous Greek writer Athenaeus. In fifteen volumes he recorded the conversations (mostly about food) and philosophy of twenty-three learned men, one of whom was Chrysippus, one of the founders of the Stoic doctrine, to whom this recipe is ascribed. Another was Galen, the famous physician of classical times. Athenaeus' account of these men's conversations gives tremendous insight into the food and dining customs of the times. The preparation and cooking of many dishes was described poetically, but seldom practically; for example: 'take a fine mullet and thrust it like a torch into the living flames'. However this sweetmeat of mixed nuts and honey is fairly clearly described, and sweetened nut cakes such as these are sold in Greece today. In ancient Greece they would have been served with wine at the end of a meal.

Makes 24 pieces

2 oz (55 g) shelled hazelnuts
2 oz (55 g) shelled walnuts
4 oz (115 g) blanched almonds

4 oz (115 g) thick honey
2 oz (55 g) sesame seeds
poppy seeds

Place all the nuts in a tin and roast in a hot oven or under the grill, watching carefully, until toasted brown. Grind them coarsely through a parsley mill or nut grater into a bowl.

Place the honey in a saucepan and bring to the boil. Remove from the heat and cool slightly. Add sufficient honey to the ground nuts to make a soft mass. With floured hands, shape the mixture into two flattish round 'cakes'.

Toast the sesame seeds under the grill and, when cooled, mix with the remaining honey until the mixture is the same consistency as the nut cakes, shape and flatten in the same way to a 'cake' of similar size. Sprinkle the top and sides with poppy seeds and gently press them in.

Sandwich the sesame seed mixture between the layers of nut mixture and press together.

Store in a tin for two days before serving to allow the cake to firm up. Then cut into fudge-sized cubes. The nut cake will keep for at least a week.

TYROPATINAM
RICHLY BAKED CUSTARD, ROMAN STYLE

The gourmet Apicius, who lived in the reign of the Emperor Tiberius, wrote down his favourite recipes, but very few written recipes for Roman desserts exist, and it is probable that fresh fruit was more the fashion than cooked 'puddings' as such. This recipe explains quite clearly how to strain the milk and egg mixture into an earthenware pot and cook over a slow fire until set. This suggests it was not stirred over direct heat but allowed to set in a slow oven.

The light sprinkling of pepper gives a slightly aromatic flavour, not unlike the nutmeg we would use today.

Serves 4-6

1 pint (600 ml) milk   *4-5 eggs*
1 tablespoon (15 ml) honey   *pinch of white pepper*

Warm the milk and honey and stir to blend. Crack the eggs into a mixing bowl and gradually whisk in the warm milk and honey. Strain into a 1½-2 pint (852 ml-1.1 litre) earthenware baking dish. Put in the centre of a slow oven (150°C, 300°F, Gas 2) and bake for 1-1½ hours or until the custard has set. Sprinkle with a pinch of pepper and serve warm or cold.

CHINESE RECIPES FROM THE SEVENTH TO THE EIGHTEENTH CENTURY

PICKLED PRAWNS FROM MADAME WU'S COOK BOOK
PRAWNS MARINATED IN RICE WINE WITH PEPPERCORNS

Madame Wu's domestic handbook called the *Chungkuei Lu* is probably the earliest Chinese cook book. It dates from the Sung Dynasty of the tenth to twelfth century AD.

Serves 4

2 lb (¾ kg) prawns
3 oz (85 g) sea salt
1 oz (30 g) table salt

¼ pint (142 ml) rice wine or dry sherry
1 tablespoon (15 ml) black peppercorns

Trim the tails and feelers off the prawns, but do not wash. Sprinkle with the sea salt and rub it in thoroughly. Leave to season for 3 hours in a refrigerator. Turn the prawns into a colander set over a deep dish to drain away the extracted water and then replace in the refrigerator again for a further 3 hours. Crush the peppercorns in a mortar just before using.

Empty the prawns into a jar. Sprinkle with the table salt, crushed peppercorns and the wine. Turn the prawns over in the mixture a few times. Seal the jar and leave the contents to stand for one week at room temperature after which time the prawns should be delicious and ready to eat.

ROYAL CONCUBINE CHICKEN
TENDER CHICKEN WITH GINGER COOKED IN A CASSEROLE

The royal concubine referred to in this case is Empress Yang Kwei-fei of the Tang Dynasty (AD 618-905). She was a great beauty but also a drunkard. In the end she was executed by the military leaders who demanded her life for having led the Emperor astray during a rebellion which eventually spelled the doom of the once-powerful Tang Dynasty. This chicken dish was named after her and could also be called 'drunken chicken', as it has a high alcohol content. The chicken should taste strongly of wine but it will be pure in flavour and tender enough to take to pieces with a pair of chopsticks – symbolic of the qualities of the royal concubine and her tragic life.

Serves 4

1 chicken, about 3 lb (1¼ kg)
2 slices root ginger
1 medium onion
2 tablespoons (30 ml) soya sauce
pepper to taste
2 stalks spring onions
oil for deep frying
1¼ pints (710 ml) chicken stock
3 level teaspoons (15 ml) salt
1½ pints (852 ml) white wine

Chop the ginger and onion coarsely and place in a bowl. Add the soya sauce and pepper to taste. Stir to blend the ingredients and then rub the chicken inside and out with the mixture. Leave for 3-4 hours to season. Cut the spring onions into ½-in (1-cm) pieces.

Have ready a large pan of boiling water. Drain the chicken and deep fry in hot oil for 7-8 minutes. Immediately immerse the chicken in the boiling water to remove all the grease. Remove the chicken straight away, place in a casserole and pour in the stock. Add the remaining ginger and onion mixture and the salt, sprinkling them over the chicken. Bring to the boil, then cover the casserole and transfer it to a moderately hot oven (190°C, 375°F, Gas 5) and cook for 45 minutes. Skim the surface of the liquid well to remove all fat and impurities. Turn the bird over, put the casserole back in the oven to cook for a further 30 minutes. Skim again, carefully removing all impurities that have risen to the surface. Add the wine and replace the casserole in the oven to cook for a final 45 minutes.

Serve in the casserole.

STIR-FRIED DICED CHICKEN CUBE WITH SHRIMPS
SPICED CHICKEN AND SHRIMPS COOKED IN WINE

This is a far more civilised dish than any of the others and is said to have dated from the time of Emperor Chien Lung's tour of south China in 1784 when he encountered and enjoyed many delicious dishes which he had not eaten before. In the northern city of Peking meats and seafoods were rarely cooked together as was common practice in the south.

Serves 2

½ lb (225 g) breast of chicken
¾ lb (340 g) shelled shrimps
1½ level teaspoons (7.5 ml) salt
2 level teaspoons (10 ml) cornflour
1 slice root ginger
1 medium onion
2 tablespoons (30 ml) vegetable oil

1 tablespoon (15 ml) sesame oil
¼ lb (115 g) green peas
2 tablespoons (30 ml) soya sauce
1½ level teaspoons (7.5 ml) sugar
2 tablespoons (30 ml) rice wine (sake) or dry sherry

Dice the chicken into ½-in (1-cm) cubes. Sprinkle with the chicken pieces and the shrimps with the salt and cornflour and rub well in. Shred the ginger and chop the onion coarsely. Heat the oil in a large frying-pan. Add the onion and ginger and stir-fry over high heat for 45 seconds. Add the chicken and stir-fry for a further 30 seconds. Add the sesame oil. Stir well and turn the mixture over a few times. Add the peas, followed by the soya sauce, sugar and wine. Continue to stir and turn for a further minute. Serve in a well-heated dish.

MONGOLIAN MEAT CAKES
AN AROMATIC MEAT, CHEESE AND ONION LOAF

Mongolian meat cakes from the Yuan Dynasty (1274-1356 or earlier) are rough-and-ready affairs with no pretensions whatever to *haute cuisine*. The blending of cheese, meats, onion, sesame oil and seeds should remind one of the flavours and aromas of the steppes of Central Asia. Quantities cooked at one time were very substantial and meat cakes would be about 1½ in thick and 12 in across. However, a more practical and civilized version of the recipe can be based on the following quantities.

Serves 4

1 lb (455 g) lean boneless lamb	*3 tablespoons (45 ml) butter or lard*
1 lb (455 g) lamb's liver and kidney	*2 tablespoons (30 ml) soya sauce*
1 large onion	*2 tablespoons (30 ml) vinegar*
1½ lb (¾ kg) potatoes or yam	*4 tablespoons (60 ml) breadcrumbs*
2 slices root ginger	*4 tablespoons (60 ml) grated goat or cow's*
2 eggs, beaten	*milk cheese — use Cheddar or Parmesan*
4 level tablespoons (60 ml) cornflour	*2 level teaspoons (10 ml) sugar*
2 level teaspoons (10 ml) salt	*2 tablespoons (30 ml) sesame seeds*
pepper to taste	*6 tablespoons (90 ml) sesame oil*

Trim and chop the lamb's meat, liver and kidney. Peel and chop the onion and potato and chop the ginger. Mix these together with the eggs, cornflour, salt, pepper, butter, soya sauce, vinegar, breadcrumbs, cheese and sugar. Mix the ingredients together thoroughly. Form the mixture into a 2-2½ in (5-6 cm) thick meat cake. Sprinkle the top with sesame seeds and press them well into the meat with the palm of the hand or the fingers.

Heat some of the sesame oil in a very large flat frying-pan and tilt the pan so that the oil runs evenly over the surface. Gently put the meat cake in the pan. Fry over medium heat for 6-7 minutes, turning once. Spoon the remaining sesame oil evenly over the top of the meat cake. Place the frying-pan under a fairly hot grill for 6-7 minutes. Using two fish slices, transfer the meat cake to a roasting tin. Set in a preheated oven (220°C, 425°F, Gas 7) and bake for 30 to 35 minutes.

To serve cut the cake into slices, there should be sufficient for 5-6 portions.

THE NOMAD'S BAKED LUNCH
TRADITIONAL SPICED LAMB WITH VEGETABLES

This recipe is derived from the Yuan or Mongol Dynasty (1279-1356). A whole, unskinned lamb with head, feet and innards removed would be wrapped in clay and cooked in a deep pit. This was probably a common method employed on the steppes of Mongolia before Mongolian habits became more civilized after they had settled in China. Something more suitable for a modern kitchen can be prepared from the following recipe which will yet retain much of the Mongolian flavour.

Serves 4-6

1 leg of lamb, about 5-6 lb (2¼-2½ kg), boned
¾ lb (340 g) lamb's kidney
1 lb (455 g) lamb's liver
2 large onions
3 lb (1¼ kg) potatoes or yams
3 slices root ginger
6 tablespoons (90 ml) soya sauce

4 tablespoons (60 ml) rice wine (sake) or dry sherry
1½ tablespoons (25 ml) soft brown sugar
black pepper to taste
4 tablespoons (60 ml) chopped parsley

Trim and chop the kidney and liver. Peel and chop the onion and potato into ½ in (1 cm) cubes. Put these in a large basin. Mince or finely chop the ginger and place in another basin with the soya sauce, wine, sugar and pepper. Mix well and add half the mixture to the prepared meat and vegetables. Rub the leg of lamb thoroughly both inside and out, with the remainder of the mixture. Leave the lamb and the stuffing to marinate for 1 hour.

Press the stuffing ingredients into the cavity in the leg of lamb. Enclose them tightly by wrapping the stuffed joint in two layers of kitchen foil. Set in a roasting tin.

Preheat the oven to very hot (230°C, 450°F, Gas 8) and place the lamb in the centre and bake for 45 minutes. Reduce the oven heat (to 200°C, 400°F, Gas 6) and cook for a further 1 hour. Finally, open out the foil, sprinkle with parsley and increase the oven temperature (to 210°C, 475°F, Gas 9) for final cooking time of 15-20 minutes. This last burst of heat will brown the mat, almost reproducing the authentic smoky flavour that you get in meat which has been cooked over an open fire or buried in or under a bonfire.

QUICK-FRIED 'THREE PARTS OF LAMB'
LAMB'S MEAT, KIDNEY AND LIVER IN A SPICED SAUCE

This dish originated in Manchuria and was introduced into Peking during the Manchu Dynasty which governed China from the 17th to the 20th century. It is a popular dish which is served in most restaurants in China and occasionally appears on menus abroad.

Serves 4

¾ lb (340 g) lean boneless lamb
½ lb (225 g) lamb's liver
½ lb (225 g) lamb's kidney
1½ level teaspoons (7.5 ml) salt
1 level tablespoon (15 ml) cornflour
2 cloves garlic

3 stalks spring onions
3 tablespoons (45 ml) sesame oil
2½ tablespoons (40 ml) soya sauce
1 tablespoon (15 ml) vinegar
1 tablespoon (15 ml) rice wine (sake) or
dry sherry

Trim and dice the lamb's meat, liver and kidney into ½-in (1-cm) cubes. Sprinkle with the salt and cornflour and rub well in. Crush and chop the garlic. Cut the spring onion into ½-in (1-cm) pieces.

Heat the sesame oil in a large frying-pan. When hot add the garlic and onion. Stir-fry quickly over high heat for ½ minute. Add the lamb's meat, kidney and liver. Continue to stir-fry for 2 minutes more. Add the soya sauce, vinegar and wine. Stir-fry for a further few minutes and serve hot.

WHITE COOKED PORK

TENDER PORK COMPLEMENTED BY GARLIC AND CHILLI DIPS

The dish originated from the Dawn and Dusk sacrifices (as well as the Sun and Moon sacrifices practised by the Manchurian court during the Ching Dynasty). A large, good-quality pig was slaughtered and served up whole for the sacrifice. When the sacrifices were over the carcass was removed to an outhouse where the court attendants and the Imperial kitchen staff proceeded to develop three types of pork dishes: 'white cooked pork' is one of them. For preparing the dish any part of the pig can be used, except the head and trotters.

Serves up to 16

10 lb (4½ kg) pork
sesame seed hot cakes (see below)

soya sauce
chilli sauce
sesame seed oil
bean curd cheese

For the dips
chopped garlic
6-12 stalks spring onions

Cut the pork into 6 in (15 cm) long and 3-4 in (7½-10 cm) wide thick pieces. Place them in a heavy iron saucepan or casserole. Cover with water and bring to the boil. Cover the pan and either place in a slow oven (150°C, 300°F, Gas 2) or set over direct heat with a simmering mat beneath for extra protection. Cook gently for 3 hours. It is important not to add any additional water once the cooking has started. After 30 minutes' cooking time, skim away all fat and impurities from the surface.

Meanwhile, crush and finely chop the garlic and cut the spring onions into ½ in (1 cm) pieces. Place them on the table in separate dishes along with the soya sauce, chilli sauce, sesame seed oil and bean curd cheese, also in separate dishes for the diners to select and mix.

When the meat is ready, allow it to cool slightly. Slice the large chunks into smaller 2 × 3 in (7½ × 7½ cm) pieces and serve. They should be eaten with toasted Peking hot cakes dipped first of all in the self-prepared dips. These hot cakes are made from ordinary flour with a small amount of baking powder, sugar and salt added. They are then covered on the outside with sesame seeds and cooked on a griddle for 7-8 min.

TUNGPO PORK
PIQUANT PORK COOKED IN A CASSEROLE

This dish is believed to have been created by one of China's greatest poets, Su Tungpo, who lived from 1036 to 1101. He was always very much preoccupied with wine and food, and is said to have created a good many dishes during the period when he was in exile.

Serves 4

2 lb (¾ kg) belly of pork
1½ level teaspoons (7.5 ml) salt
3 stalks spring onions
2 slices root ginger

2 tablespoons (30 ml) soya sauce
4 tablespoons (60 ml) rice wine (sake) or dry sherry
1½ level teaspoons (7.5 ml) sugar

Cut the pork through the skin into squares at 1 in (2.5 cm) intervals. Sprinkle the pork with the salt, rub in well and leave to season for 3 hours. Drain the liquid from the pork and parboil the pieces in boiling water for 15 minutes. Remove the meat with a slotted spoon. Pour away the water and parboil a second time in fresh boiling water for a further 15 minutes. Cut the spring onions into ½-in (1-cm) pieces. Peel and shred the ginger.

Pack the pork, skin side down, in a casserole. Mix the soya sauce, wine, sugar, spring onion and shredded ginger in a bowl. Sprinkle the mixture evenly over the pork. Bring the mixture to a simmer over direct heat, then cover with a tight-fitting lid and put the casserole in a slow oven (150°C, 300°F, Gas 2) and cook for 2 hours.

Turn the pork out of the casserole into a deep-sided heatproof dish, skin side up. Cover tightly with a piece of kitchen foil and place the dish in a steamer. Steam steadily for 1½ hours. Remove the foil and serve in the dish. The pork should be as tender as jelly.

PERSIAN AND INDIAN RECIPES FROM THE THIRTEENTH TO THE NINETEENTH CENTURY

El Baghdadi, author of the famours 13th-century manual on cooking and food, often began his recipes with the intriguing instructions to 'melt fresh tail' or 'dissolve the tail' and throw away the sediment. The resulting oil was used for frying meat. Even today, the tails of Middle Eastern sheep are not docked as ours are to prevent much of the animal's fat going into the tail, and the tail would have provided a plentiful supply of cooking fat. Instructions are given below for clarifying lamb dripping, which gives an absolutely clear oil for frying.

Small pastries and sweet loaves were often dipped into scented syrup, a recipe for which is given below. The syrup should be thoroughly chilled so that when hot pastry or bread is dipped into it the syrup instantly forms a thin glaze. Scented sugar was also used for making pastries and breads and for dusting over them. Most cooks nowadays keep a jar of scented sugar in their store cupboard for making cakes.

In the Indian recipes reference is constantly made to ghee and also to tyre. Ghee is clarified butter and can be bought in tins from most Asian stores, but it is very easy to make at home and will keep indefinitely. Tyre was made by adding a little buttermilk to warm fresh milk and letting it stand all night; in a hot climate the mixture would have soured by the morning, so we give a combination of soured cream and milk as a substitute. Finally, as well as many of the spices used in the Roman and medieval recipes, turmeric is also needed and some dishes call for fresh ginger which can be bought from some greengrocers, health shops and Asian stores. The sliced root of green ginger is also sold in small tins. As in the preceding recipes, almonds, pine kernels and pistachio nuts are also used.

Here are the ingredients you may need to prepare yourself for some of the recipes.

SCENTED SYRUP

½ lb (225 g) caster sugar
¼ pint (142 ml) water
juice of ½ lemon

2 teaspoons (10 ml) rosewater
2 teaspoons (10 ml) orange flower water

Put the sugar, water and lemon juice into a saucepan. Bring slowly to the boil, stirring well until the sugar has dissolved and skimming off any froth as it rises. Boil briskly without a lid for 10 minutes. Add one or both of the perfumed waters and boil together for 2 minutes more. Cool and chill. This syrup will keep indefinitely in a bottle or screw-topped jar in the refrigerator.

SCENTED SUGAR

Store caster sugar in a screw-topped jar with a vanilla pod or piece of cinnamon stick, or both. (Camphor and musk were also used for scented sugars but these would seem rather strange to our tastes.)

CLARIFIED LAMB DRIPPING

Heat the dripping saved from roast lamb gently in a pan. Pour through a strainer to remove the sediment and use the remaining oil for frying. When cool, store in the refrigerator.

GHEE

Melt a good quantity of unsalted butter in a heavy pan over a low heat. When the whitish lumps of curd that rise to the top begin to turn brown remove the pan from the heat and strain through a double thickness of muslin (discard the sediment). When cool, pour into a clean screw-topped jar and store in the refrigerator. The ghee will keep indefinitely if stored in this way.

TYRE

Take 4 tablespoons (60 ml) of soured cream and twice the amount of fresh milk. Mix together and use as directed in in the recipes.

MALIH BI KHALLWA-KHARDEL
SMOKED FISH COOKED WITH VINEGAR AND MUSTARD

The original medieval dish called for salted fish which being hard and dry would require long soaking. Smoked haddock makes an excellent modern substitute. The dish of plain rice absorbs the juices and it is delicious hot, but is also good cold if the haddock is flaked, mixed with a little rice and served with a salad. El Baghadi, the author of this recipe wrote a manual on cooking in 1226 which was not rediscovered until 1934. Professor Arberry, the famous Arabist, translated the manuscript of recipes which give a fascinating insight into the ideas and customs of the times. To El Baghdadi, pleasures were divided into six classes 'to wit, food, drink, clothes, sex, scent and sound. Of these, the oldest and most consequential is food; for food is the body's stay, and the means of preserving life'. He goes on to say 'I subscribe to the doctrine of the preexcellence of the pleasure of eating above all other pleasures and for that reason I have composed this book ...'

Serves 4

2-3 tablespoons (30-45 ml) sesame oil
4 fillets smoked haddock, about 1½-2 lb (¾-1 kg)
4 tablespoons (60 ml) white wine vinegar

¼ level teaspoon (1.25 ml) dry mustard powder
2 teaspoons (10 ml) ground coriander
pinch powdered saffron

Heat the oil in a frying-pan and fry the haddock fillets until lightly browned on both sides. Discard any surplus oil and pour over 3 tablespoons (45 ml) of the vinegar. Mix the remaining tablespoonful (15 ml) vinegar with the mustard and add to the fish, along with the coriander and saffron. Cover and cook gently for 10 minutes. Remove the lid and finish cooking for a further 5 minutes. Serve the haddock on a bed of rice with all the juices poured over.

SHIRAZ BI BUQAL
COTTAGE CHEESE WITH WALNUTS AND FRESH HERBS

The old Persian recipe describes this as 'an excellent relish which both awakens and stimulates the appetite'. It recommends dried curds or coagulated milk, for which we have substituted cottage cheese. The flavouring of chopped celery leaves, mint and leeks sharpened with mustard is deliciously original, and the topping of walnuts looks as good as it tastes. The dish would probably have been eaten for the first meal of the day when fruit, milk, cheese and preserves were served between 10 and 11 in the morning.

Serves 4-6

½ teaspoon (2.5 ml) chopped fresh mint
1 heaped tablespoon (17.25 ml) chopped
leek (white part only)
1 heaped tablespoon (17.25 ml) chopped
celery leaves
8 oz (225 g) cottage cheese

pinch salt
pinch dry mustard powder
10 or 12 coarsely chopped walnut halves

Put the mint, leek and celery leaves through a parsley mill, or chop very finely. Stir into the cottage cheese with the salt and mustard.

Heap the mixture into a small earthenware dish and sprinkle over the chopped walnuts. Serve with bread or crispbread.

LAHMA BI AJEEN
ARAB BREAD WITH SAVOURY BEEF AND ONION FILLING

This is a traditional Arab dish which if translated literally means 'meat and bread'. The result is small individual pizza-type savouries that are succulent and delicately spiced and which, when folded in half, are easy to eat in the fingers.

Serves 4

6 oz (170 g) plain flour
½ level teaspoon (2.5 ml) salt
scant ¼ pint (142 ml) water
pinch sugar
2 level teaspoons (10 ml) dried yeast
scant tablespoon (7.25 ml) sesame or vegetable oil

For the topping
1 large onion
1 tablespoon (15 ml) sesame or vegetable oil
½ lb (225 g) minced beef
1 level teaspoon (5 ml) salt
freshly milled black pepper
1 tablespoon (15 ml) chopped parsley or dill, or other fresh herbs
¼ level teaspoon (1.25 ml) ground allspice
1 heaped tablespoon (17.25) ground almonds
1 teaspoon (5 ml) sugar
1 tablespoon (15 ml) lemon juice

Sift the flour and salt into a warmed mixing basin. Heat the water until a little hotter than lukewarm – almost 110°F (55°C) or hand hot. Stir in the sugar and sprinkle in the dried yeast. Set aside in a warm place for about 10 minutes or until the yeast is frothy.

Pour the yeast liquid into the centre of the flour and add the oil. Stir with a wooden spoon to blend the ingredients, then mix by hand to a rough dough. Turn out on to a clean working surface and knead very well for about 15 minutes until the dough is smooth and soft. Put it back in the basin, cover and leave in a warm place until it has doubled in size.

Meanwhile, prepare the meat topping. Finely chop the onion and fry gently in the hot oil to soften, but do not allow it to brown. Put the minced beef in a mixing basin. Add the cooked onion, salt, pepper, herbs, allspice, ground

PERSIAN AND INDIAN RECIPES FROM THE 13TH TO THE 19TH CENTURY .

almonds, sugar and lemon juice. Mix well by hand to get a smooth mixture.

Turn out the risen dough and press all over with the knuckles to knock out the air. Take small pieces of the dough, about the size of a walnut, and flatten with the heel of your hand to make circles about 4-5 in (10-13 cm) in diameter. Pile a generous quantity of the meat filling on each one and spread over the surface. Place on lightly oiled baking trays. Set in a very hot oven (230°C, 450°F, Gas 8) and bake for about 8 minutes until the dough is just cooked, but still soft (not browned). Serve hot. Fold each pastry in half to eat.

DOEPEAZA DILAEE KHANEE
RICH BEEF STEW WITH CREAMY ALMOND SAUCE

The spices in this dish give a faint and subtle taste of curry without the hotness while the creamy sauce flavoured with onions and almonds adds a rich taste and texture. The small whole onions called for in the original recipe are a worthwhile addition to this fragrant stew.

Serves 4

1 lb (455 g) lean stewing steak
12 cloves
5 cardamom pods
plenty of freshly milled black pepper
1 teaspoon (5 ml) ground cinnamon
2 teaspoons (10 ml) turmeric
1 heaped tablespoon (17.25 ml) sour cream mixed with 2 tablespoons (30 ml) milk
6 oz (170 g) ghee (page 35)

½ pint (284 ml) warm water
1 large onion
pinch saffron strands soaked in 2 tablespoons (30 ml) hot water
6 small whole onions, or shallots
salt
2 oz (55 g) ground almonds
1 tablespoon (15 ml) cream

Trim the meat and cut into thin slices. Crush the cloves and the cardamom pods and place in a basin with the pepper, cinnamon and turmeric. Stir in the soured cream and milk and blend well. Add the slices of meat and turn them in the mixture to coat well.

Heat a little more than half the ghee in a large saucepan. Add the pieces of meat and fry gently until brown on both sides. Pour the warm water into the bowl which contained the spice and sour cream mixture, stir well to blend in any remaining mixture and then pour over the meat in the saucepan. Cover with a lid and simmer gently over low heat for 1 hour.

Meanwhile peel and thinly slice the large onion. Fry gently in the remaining ghee until tender and golden brown. Stir in the infused saffron and the water in which it soaked. Set aside.

Peel the small onions, leaving them whole. Prick them all over with a fork and rub them well with salt (preferably ground salt crystals). Remove the lid from the pan of meat and add the whole onions. Allow to simmer gently, uncovered for a further 30 minutes or until the meat is tender.

Before serving, take out about ¼ pint (142 ml) of the

cooking liquid from the meat and blend it with the ground almonds and the cream. Pour over the meat and add the fried onion and saffron mixture. Simmer gently together for 5-10 minutes. Serve hot with rice as an accompaniment.

DAKSHINI CHAAVAL
LIGHT, FLUFFY RICE

This method of cooking rice is traditional in Southern India and results in a very light, fluffy rice which goes well with all spicy dishes.

Serves 6

¾ lb (340 g) long grain rice
5 pints (3 litres) water
½ tablespoon salt
2 oz (50 g) melted ghee

Wash the rice in several changes of cold water, then leave to drain for 10 minutes. Bring the 5 pints (3 litres) water to the boil, add the salt and slowly pour in the rice, so that the water does not go off the boil. Boil fast for 7 minutes in the uncovered pan, then drain through a fine sieve. Tip the rice into a large earthenware pot with a lid, trickle the melted ghee over the rice and cover the pot with foil and the lid. Put in a slow oven (150°, 300°F, Gas 2) for 30 minutes and stir lightly with a fork before serving.

MUQARRASA
FRIED MEAT BALLS WITH GARLIC AND SPICE

A bowl of rice is a suitable accompaniment to these savoury little meat cakes in their spicy juices. Being all meat they are quite filling and, surprisingly, they do hold together in the pan even though they have no flour or egg to bind them.

The cakes would have been cooked over a fire of charcoal, wood or even dried dung. El Baghdadi wrote that the best woods to use for cooking were olive or ilex; above all he advised avoiding the wood of the fig tree which emitted too much acrid smoke.

Serves 4

1 lb (455 g) lean beef
3-4 cloves garlic
1 level teaspoon (5 ml) salt
½ level teaspoon (2.5 ml) freshly milled
black pepper
2 tablespoons (30 ml) clarified lamb
dripping (page 35)

4 tablespoons (60 ml) warm water
1 tablespoon (15 ml) ground coriander
1 level teaspoon (5 ml) ground cumin
1 level teaspoon (5 ml) ground cinnamon

Trim the meat and cut in pieces. Mince it finely along with the garlic. Place in a basin and season with the salt and pepper. Beat and mix the ingredients well to bind together. Using wetted hands shape spoonfuls of the mixture into balls – you should get about 10 balls. Flatten each one into a round patty.

Heat the dripping in the frying-pan. Add the meat cakes and fry them until brown on both sides. Pour away surplus fat and add the water. Simmer gently, uncovered, until the liquid has nearly all evaporated. Sprinkle with the coriander, cumin and cinnamon. Cover with a lid and leave over a very low heat for an hour, or until ready to serve.

SHURBA
LAMB AND CHICK PEAS WITH SPICED RICE

This is a very aromatic dish with a good, distinctive flavour. The chick-peas are delicious and unusual and as the dish is cooked with well-spiced rice, it is a meal on its own. Finely shredded cabbage cooked in a little wine, or vinegar and water, with a few caraway seeds, goes well with it.

Most of the early Persian recipes advised keeping the dish warm over a low heat before serving, the flavour is mellowed and improved if it is not served straight away. Often, as in this recipe, the cooking pot was wiped round with a clean cloth dipped in rosewater before it was set aside to keep warm.

Serves 4

2 lb (910 g) boned shoulder or leg of lamb
¼ lb (115 g) clarified lamb dripping (page 35)
½ pint (284 ml) lukewarm water
2 oz (55 g) chick-peas, soaked overnight
2 in (5 cm) long piece of cinnamon stick
1 level teaspoon (5 ml) salt
2 heaped teaspoons (6.25 ml) dried dill

For the rice
6 oz (165 g) long-grain rice
½ pint (284 ml) lukewarm water
¼ level teaspoon (1.25 ml) freshly milled black pepper
1 level teaspoon (5 ml) ground ginger
1 tablespoon (15 ml) ground coriander
1 teaspoon (5 ml) ground cumin
1 teaspoon (5 ml) ground cinnamon

Trim and cut the meat into small pieces. Heat the dripping in a large saucepan, add the meat and brown all over. Drain off the surplus fat and pour in the water – there should be just sufficient to cover the meat. Add the chick-peas, cinnamon, salt and dill. Cover the pan and cook gently for 1½ hours or until the meat is tender.

Wash the rice and add to the pan of meat with the water, pepper, ginger and coriander. Bring to the boil, cover and cook gently until the rice is tender. Taste and add more salt if necessary. Sprinkle with the cumin and cinnamon and set over a very low heat until ready to serve. A simmering mat is very useful to prevent scorching and you may safely leave it for an hour.

MUJADDARA
SPICY LAMB WITH RICE AND LENTILS

A dish which combines the earthy flavour of lentils with fragrantly spicy meat. The result should be dry without being dried out, all the liquids having been absorbed in the gentle process of cooking.

El Baghdadi preferred cooking pots of stone above all others, then earthenware and, as a last resort, they could be of tinned copper, but there was nothing more abominable, he said, than food cooked in a copper pot which had lost its tinning. For an authentic touch, you could cook and serve this dish in a heavy earthenware or stoneware pot.

Serves 4

4 oz (115 g) brown or yellow lentils
2 lb (1 kg) lean lamb, boned
2 tablespoons (30 ml) clarified lamb dripping (page 35)
1 tablespoon (30 ml) ground coriander
2 level teaspoons (30 ml) salt

1 teaspoon (30 ml) ground cumin
1 teaspoon (30 ml) ground cinnamon
8 oz (225 g) long-grain rice, washed
1 in (2½ cm) long piece cinnamon stick, crushed
water, see recipe

Wash the lentils well and drain, then cook in fresh, unsalted water for about 30 minutes, or until soft. Drain and set aside.

Cut the meat into cubes. Heat 1 tablespoon (15 ml) of the dripping in a heavy pan and add the meat. Brown the pieces on all sides. Add the coriander and 1 teaspoon (5 ml) salt and pour in sufficient water to just cover the meat. Bring up to the boil and skim. Add the cumin and cinnamon, cover and allow to simmer for at least 1 hour. The meat should be very tender and the water should have evaporated. If any liquid remains, remove the pan lid and simmer a little longer until it has all been absorbed.

Heat the remaining dripping in a second saucepan. Add the cooked lentils and the rice, the remaining teaspoon (5 ml) salt and crushed cinnamon stick. Pour in about 1 pint (568 ml) water and bring to the boil. Cover and simmer for 20 minutes until the rice is cooked and the water has been absorbed. Halfway through the cooking time, check that the rice is neither sticking nor too dry; add more water if necessary.

Check the seasoning of the cooked rice and lentils, then put the cooked meat on top. Cover the pan with a cloth and a tightly fitting lid and leave over a very gentle heat, or remove from the heat and stand in a warm place for a further 30 minutes. This dish will not spoil if kept a little longer.

KULLEAH KOONDUM
LAMB CURRY WITH SAVOURY EGGS

A fragrant, curry-flavoured stew topped with hard-boiled eggs, each of which is wrapped in a spicy meat jacket. If you want to serve a whole egg for each person (instead of half each), buy ¼ lb (115 g) more meat for mincing and increase the onion and spices a little. You can vary the proportions of spices according to taste, but always make sure they enhance, rather than overpower, the flavour of the meat in this nineteenth century Indian recipe.

Serves 4

1½ lb (¾ kg) lamb, boned
1 lb (455 g) onions
¼ teaspoon (1.25 ml) ground cloves
1 teaspoon (5 ml) ground cinnamon
1 tablespoon (15 ml) ground coriander
1 teaspoon (5 ml) ground ginger

4 oz (115 g) ghee (page 35)
¼ pint (142 ml) water
1 tablespoon (15 ml) flaked almonds
2 hard-boiled eggs
flour
squeeze lemon or lime juice

Trim all the meat and finely mince ¼ lb (115 g) of it. Finely chop 6 oz (170 g) of the onions and mix the minced meat and onions together. Mix the cloves, cinnamon, coriander and ginger in a small basin. Heat a little of the ghee in a frying-pan. Add the minced meat and onion mixture and 1 heaped teaspoon (6.25 ml) of the spice mixture from the small basin. Fry all together until the onions are soft, but not browned. Turn into a basin and set aside. Reserve any juices in the pan.

Cube the rest of the meat and slice the remaining onions. Heat a little of the remaining ghee in a saucepan. Add the meat pieces, the sliced onion, the remaining spice mixture and any juices remaining in the frying-pan after cooking the minced meat and onion mixture. Stir over the heat until the ingredients are blended and beginning to brown. Add the water and bring to the boil. Cover and cook gently for 45 minutes. Add the flaked almonds and cook for a further 5 minutes.

Meanwhile, pass the fried meat and onion mixture twice through a fine mincer. Squeeze the mixture to a paste in your hand. Shell the hard-boiled eggs and prick them all over with a fork. Divide the meat mixture equally in half and flatten out each one on a floured surface. Wrap a portion round each egg. Roll the eggs lightly in flour and fry them carefully in the remaining ghee. Cut the eggs in half lengthways, allowing half an egg per person. Dish the curry stew with a squeeze of lemon or lime juice over it. Put the halved eggs on top and serve with a dish of plain rice, or with the traditional Indian dish of spiced rice given below.

MASALEDAR BASMATI
TRADITIONAL SPICED RICE

Serves 4

10 oz (285 g) Basmati rice
2 tablespoons (30 ml) vegetable oil
2 oz (55 g) onion, finely chopped
½ fresh green chilli, de-seeded and chopped
1 teaspoon (5 ml) garlic, crushed

2 cloves, crushed
2 cardamom pods, crushed
½ teaspoon (2.5 ml) ground cumin
½ teaspoon (2.5 ml) ground cinnamon
1 teaspoon (5 ml) salt
1 pint (568 g) chicken stock

Wash the rice in several changes of cold water, then leave to soak in fresh water for 30 minutes. Allow to drain for 10 minutes. Heat the oil in a heavy saucepan, add the onion and fry gently until light brown. Add the rice, green chilli, garlic, spices and salt. Stir together for a few minutes until the rice is well coated with oil, stir in the stock and bring to the boil, then cover with a well-fitting lid, or foil under the lid, and cook over a very low heat for 25 minutes. Keep the pan covered throughout the cooking time, so that no steam escapes.

UNUNASS PULLOW
SWEET-SOUR LAMB WITH RICE AND PINEAPPLE

This is a very delicious sweet-sour Indian dish. Half the flesh of a small fresh pineapple is cooked in a light sugar syrup for a final garnish to the meat; the other half is cooked, with spices added to the syrup, until it is brown and sticky, then combined with the meat to give a fresh chutney flavour. For a hot climate, this spicy-sweet flavour stimulates the appetite and on a sultry day gives energy to the diners. Serve with a cooling dish of diced cucumber and finely chopped onion stirred into plenty of plain yoghurt, seasoned with salt and pepper, and with a little finely chopped mint scattered over the top.

Serves 4

1½ lb (¾ kg) lean lamb, boned
1 large onion
¾ pint (426 ml) water
2 slices fresh ginger, peeled and cut into narrow strips
1 level teaspoon (5 ml) salt
1 tablespoon (15 ml) ground coriander
¼ lb (115 g) ghee (page 35)
2 cloves

For the pineapple and spiced syrup mixture
2 oz (55 g) caster sugar
½ pint (284 ml) water
juice of ½ lemon
1 small fresh pineapple
½ level teaspoon (2.5 ml) ground cloves
1 teaspoon (5 ml) cumin seeds
3 cardamom pods, crushed
1 level teaspoon (5 ml) ground cinnamon
6 oz (170 g) long-grain rice

Trim and cut the meat into small, thick slices. Peel and slice the onion. Place the meat, onion, water, ginger strips, salt, coriander and 1 tablespoon (15 ml) of the ghee in a saucepan. Bring to the boil, cover and simmer for 1 hour. When cooked strain the juices from the meat into another saucepan and set aside for cooking the rice. Heat 2 tablespoons (30 ml) of the remaining ghee in a large frying-pan with the cloves. Add the meat and onion mixture and allow to fry gently until the mixture begins to brown. Turn the meat pieces to fry on each side.

Meanwhile, prepare the pineapple mixture. Dissolve the sugar in the water and lemon juice and bring to the boil. Cut the rind off the pineapple and cut the flesh into slices. Put half the pineapple slices into the syrup, cover and boil for 15 minutes. Remove the fruit and reserve for the garnish. Add the remaining pineapple slices to the syrup, this time with the ground cloves, the cumin seeds, the crushed cardamom pods and the cinnamon. Boil, uncovered, until the syrup has nearly all evaporated and the mixture is sticky and brown.

Transfer the meat and onions from the frying-pan to the saucepan of spicy pineapple. Stir together and keep over a low heat. Bring the juices that were reserved for cooking the rice to the boil; add the washed rice, cover and cook for 15 minutes. The gravy should all be absorbed by the rice.

Dish up the meat and spoon the cooked rice over. Pour over the melted ghee – about 1 tablespoon (15 ml) of the original quantity should remain. Garnish with the cooked pineapple slices and serve hot.

KOOKRA PULLOW
SPICY ROAST CHICKEN WITH SAVOURY MEAT BALLS

This may sound a complicated recipe, but it is not difficult to make if you have all the ingredients ready. There is plenty of time to make the meatballs and cook the eggs and rice while the chicken is roasting. It is a beautiful-looking dish with a combination of subtle flavours – and the pan juices are wonderfully rich and creamy. The recipe comes from an enlightened English woman who, rather than attempting to recreate the menus from home, made a study of Indian food and cooking methods and wrote a book which included not only recipes, but advice on household management, horticulture, health and the treatment of sickness in animals and people.

Serves 6

*1 roasting chicken, about 3½-4½ lb
(1½-2 kg)
1 lb (455 g) lean lamb, boned
salt
1 tablespoon (15 ml) ground coriander
1 medium onion
1 teaspoon (5 ml) ground ginger
4 cardamom pods
4 whole cloves
4 tablespoons (60 ml) soured cream
mixed with 5 tablespoons (75 ml) milk*

*pinch powdered saffron
1 oz (30 g) butter
3 slices fresh ginger, peeled
½ level teaspoon (2.5 ml) ground
cinnamon
pinch salt
freshly milled black pepper
3 eggs
¼ lb (115 g) ghee (page 35)
4 oz (115 g) long-grain rice*

Wipe the chicken well inside and set aside while preparing the stuffing. Cut up and mince about 6 oz (170 g) of the lamb. Mix with a pinch of salt and half the coriander. Stuff this mixture inside the chicken. Peel and halve the onion and rub the cut surface of the onion over the chicken; reserve the onion for later in the recipe. Rub the chicken all over with the ground ginger. Crush two of the cardamom pods and two of the cloves. Mix with the soured cream and milk and the saffron to make a sauce for basting. Grease the inside of a roasting tin with the butter. Place the chicken in the tin and spread with a little of the basting sauce. Roast in a hot oven (200°C, 400°F, Gas 6) for 1½ hours, basting with the remaining sauce about 4 times during the cooking time.

Mince the rest of the lamb with 2 slices of the fresh ginger and place in a mixing basin. Add half the cinnamon and half the pepper, a good seasoning of salt and the remaining ½ teaspoon (2.5 ml) of ground coriander. Stir in 1 egg white – taken from the 3 eggs, and mix by hand, squeezing the ingredients to a paste. Using wetted hands, shape spoonfuls of the mixture into about 12 small meat balls. Flatten each one a little and fry in about 2 tablespoons (30 ml) of the ghee until they are brown on all sides. Remove the meatballs from the pan and reserve the pan drippings.

Finely slice the reserved onion and the remaining slice of ginger. Mix in a bowl with the 2 whole eggs and the egg yolk. Add a little salt and pepper and mix well with a fork. If necessary add a little more ghee to the pan in which you fried the meat balls and when hot, add the egg and onion mixture. Stir with a fork as if making an omelette. Cook gently until the eggs have set firm, then remove from the heat.

Wash the rice thoroughly and drain well. Add to a pan of boiling salted water along with the remaining cloves, cardamom pods and pepper. Boil for 10 minutes until the rice is barely tender, then drain well.

Return the rice to the saucepan and on top place the meat balls, and the egg and onion mixture, cut into pieces about 1 in (2.5 cm) square. Pour the rest of the ghee and 2 tablespoons (30 ml) of the juices taken from the roasting chicken over the contents of the saucepan. Cover closely with a tight-fitting lid, or foil and lid, and cook gently for 10-15 minutes until the rice is quite tender and the meat balls and egg mixture heated through.

Spoon contents of the pan on to a serving dish. Dish up the chicken separately and pour every scrap of the delicious juices from the tin over the bird.

KUBAB FOWL OR MEAT
CHICKEN IN CREAMY ALMOND AND ONION SAUCE

The chicken in this Indian recipe is first rubbed with powdered spices, and then basted during roasting with a delicious cream and onion sauce, flavoured with turmeric. The mixture has a gentle curry flavour, far more subtle than any of the hot-tasting ready-made curry powders give. The original recipe suggests that a shoulder of mutton or lamb can also be prepared this way.

Serves 4-6

1 roasting chicken, about 4 lb (1¾ kg)
1 tablespoon (15 ml) ground coriander
1 teaspoon (5 ml) ground ginger
crushed seeds from 4 cardamom pods
3 cloves, crushed
plenty of freshly milled black pepper
1 level teaspoon (5 ml) salt
1 oz (30 g) ghee (page 35), for roasting

For the basting mixture
1 medium onion
2 oz (55 g) ghee (page 35)
3 teaspoons (15 ml) turmeric
2 tablespoons (10 ml) flaked almonds
1 tablespoon (15 ml) currants
2 heaped tablespoons (17.25 ml) double cream
2 heaped tablespoons (17.25 ml) soured cream mixed with 4 tablespoons (60 ml) milk

Prick the chicken all over with a sharp knife. Mix together the coriander, ginger, crushed cardamom seeds, crushed cloves, pepper and salt. Rub this mixture all over the chicken. Put the chicken in a roasting tin with the 1 oz (30 g) ghee. Place in a moderately hot oven (190°C, 375°F, Gas 5) to roast.

Meanwhile, prepare the basting sauce. Peel and slice the onion and fry in the ghee with the turmeric until the onion is soft but not brown. Stir in the almonds and currants. Add the fresh cream with the soured cream and milk mixture. Stir thoroughly together and remove from the heat.

When the chicken has been roasting for 20 minutes, baste with half the onion and cream mixture. After another 10 minutes, baste again with the rest of the mixture and reduce the oven temperature if the chicken is browning too quickly. Baste again once or twice with the juices in the tin during the total cooking time of 1½ hours. Serve on a hot dish with all the sauce from the roasting tin poured over the chicken.

BASBOUSA BIL LOZ
A PERSIAN SWEET WITH ALMONDS AND LEMON

Here is a delicate little sweet, made with semolina and tasting of almonds and lemon. Semolina, ground rice and cornflour are all used in the making of these creamy desserts in the Middle East today; sometimes they are flavoured with cinnamon, sometimes delicately perfumed with rose-water, or orange-flower water. Almonds or pistachio nuts may be used as a garnish, and nuts and raisins are sometimes stirred in to the thickened mixture. Serve this dessert cool but not chilled in small china or earthenware pots. A few toasted almonds, or a spoonful of whipped cream, or both, make an attractive topping to each pot. Originally the cream used for decoration would have been *eishta*, made from buffaloes' milk, which was boiled until the cream on it became thick enough to cut with a knife. Clotted cream, or thickly whipped double cream, makes an acceptable substitute.

Serves 4

6 oz (170 g) caster sugar
¾ pint (426 ml) water
juice of 1 lemon
3 oz (85 g) butter

2 oz (55 g) blanched and chopped
almonds
2 oz (55 g) semolina

Heat the sugar, water and lemon juice in a pan. Stir until the sugar is dissolved, then boil for 3 minutes.

Melt the butter in a second saucepan, add the almonds and semolina. Stir together and fry gently until golden. Stir in the syrup slowly and cook over gentle heat until the mixture thickens – this takes about 5 minutes. Remove from the heat and allow to cool for a few moments, stirring occasionally to prevent a skin forming. Pour into small individual pots and serve.

SANBUSAJ AND SANBUNIYA
SMALL PASTRIES WITH SAVOURY OR SWEET FILLING

These two recipes, one savoury and the second sweet can be made from the same dough. *Sanbusaj* are little triangles of pastry stuffed with minced beef, flavoured with spices, lemon and chopped walnuts. Sanbuniya should be even tinier triangles or half-circles of pastry stuffed with a sweet-scented almond paste and while hot dipped in cold syrup and dusted with scented sugar. They are such dainty and delicious morsels that at a banquet in the tenth century given by the Caliph of Baghdad, a poem was recited describing the delights of *sanbusaj*.

Makes about 30 small pastries

For the pastry dough

1 lb (455 g) plain flour	5 tablespoons (75 ml) warm water
4 oz (115 g) butter	pinch salt
6 tablespoons (90 ml) sesame oil	

Sift the flour. Put the butter and oil in a large mixing basin and set over a saucepan of hot water to allow the butter to melt. Stir in the water and the salt. Remove the basin from the heat and gradually stir in the flour. The mixture will form a soft, greasy ball. Do not handle too much.
    Set aside in a cool place while preparing the fillings.

Savoury filling for the Sanbusaj

½ lb (225 g) minced beef	½ teaspoon (2.5 ml) crushed cumin seeds
5 tablespoons (75 ml) water	pinch dried mint
squeeze lemon juice	1 oz (30 g) walnuts, chopped
salt and freshly milled black pepper	1 small egg, lightly beaten
3 teaspoons (15 ml) ground coriander	oil for frying

Place the minced beef, water, lemon juice and a good seasoning of salt and pepper in a saucepan. Add the coriander, cumin and dried mint. Cover and simmer gently for about 15 minutes. Towards the end of the cooking time, remove the lid and allow any excess liquid to evaporate. The meat should be moist, but not wet. Add the walnuts and stir well. Remove the pan from the heat and stir in the egg. Return to the heat and stir until the egg has thickened. Allow the mixture to cool.

Take half the quantity of pastry dough and roll out very thinly on a floured surface. Cut into 3-in (7½-cm) squares. Place a spoonful of the filling on one side of each and fold into neat triangles. Trim, if necessary, and pinch together, lightly. Place on a lightly oiled baking tray, set in a moderate oven (180°C, 350°F, Gas 4) and bake for 30 minutes; or shallow fry gently in hot oil until golden on each side. Drain on absorbent paper. Eat hot or cold.

Mukallal filling for Sanbuniya

2 oz (55 g) ground almonds	*oil for frying*
2 oz (55 g) caster sugar	*scented syrup (page 35)*
4 teaspoons (20 ml) rosewater	*scented sugar (page 35)*

Put the ground almonds, sugar and rosewater into a bowl and stir them together.

Take half the quantity of pastry dough and roll out very thinly on a floured surface. Cut in small squares of about 2 in (5 cm), or stamp out circles with a rounded pastry cutter. Put teaspoonsfuls (5 ml) of the filling into the centre of each. Fold over into tiny half-triangles or half-circles and seal the edges together carefully.

Place on a lightly oiled baking tray, set in a moderate oven (180°C, 350°F, Gas 4) and bake for 30 minutes; or shallow fry in hot oil until golden brown on both sides. Drain on absorbent paper. While still hot, dip into scented syrup and dust with scented sugar. Eat cold.

AQRAS MUKALLALA
BREAD WITH A SWEET NUT-PASTE FILLING

These are small, soft, white loaves which are filled with a sweet pistachio paste or almond paste. As soon as they come from the oven they are dipped in cold scented syrup and rolled in scented sugar. This does not leave them heavily sticky; the hot bread only absorbs a thin sheen of syrup. When sliced diagonally, the line of green pistachio filling shows prettily in each slice. Make the scented syrup well in advance so that it is thoroughly chilled. Although such an elegant and sophisticated recipe, it dates back to medieval times and is Persian in origin.

Makes 4 small loaves

½ lb (225 g) plain flour
1 level teaspoon (5 ml) salt
¼ pint (142 ml) milk and water mixed in equal parts
1 level teaspoon (5 ml) sugar

2 level teaspoons (10 ml) dried yeast
1 tablespoon (15 ml) sesame oil
pistachio paste (see recipe, below)
scented syrup (page 35)
scented sugar (page 35)

Sift the flour and salt into a warmed mixing basin. Heat the milk and water to about 110°F (55°C) or hand hot. Stir in the sugar and sprinkle in the dried yeast. Set aside in a warm place for about 10 minutes or until the yeast is frothy.

Pour the yeast liquid into the centre of the flour and add the oil. Stir with a wooden spoon to blend the ingredients, then mix by hand in the basin to a rough dough. Turn out and knead very well for about 5 minutes until the dough is smooth and soft. Replace in the basin, cover and leave in a warm place until double in size.

Meanwhile, prepare the pistachio or almond paste according to the recipes given below.

Turn the risen dough out, press all over with the knuckles to knock out the air and divide into 4 pieces. Roll each piece out to a 'rope' of about 6 in (15 cm), and flatten with the hand. Roll a portion of the pistachio paste to a thinner rope of the same length and place one down the centre of each portion of dough. Fold the dough over and pinch the edges together to seal. Place the loaves on an oiled baking tray with the sealed edges underneath. Leave in a warm place to prove until puffy. Set in a very hot oven (230°C, 450°F, Gas 8) and bake for 20 minutes. Remove each loaf from the oven and dip immediately into the cold scented syrup. Roll in scented sugar and leave to cool.

Pistachio paste

2 oz (55 g) whole pistachio nuts   4 teaspoons (20 ml) scented syrup (page
2 oz (55 g) caster sugar   35)

Blanch the nuts in boiling water, drain and remove the skins. Pass the nuts through a nut mill to grate finely. Mix the nuts, sugar and enough scented syrup together to make a stiff paste.

Almond paste (Khushkranaj)

2 oz (55 g) ground almonds   4 teaspoons (20 ml) rosewater
2 oz (55 g) scented sugar (page 35)

Almond filling makes a delicious alternative to pistachio, although it is not so attractively coloured. Measure the ground almonds, sugar and rosewater into a basin. Mix the ingredients together to make a stiff paste.

ENGLISH RECIPES FROM THE FOURTEENTH TO THE NINETEENTH CENTURY

As with the Roman garum, medieval dishes often call for almond milk as a special ingredient. Its flavour adds a delicate fragrance to sauces, whether savoury or sweet. Although now lost to western cooking, almond milk is still made in the Middle East, where it is diluted with ice-cold water and taken as a refreshing drink. Simple instructions for making it from ground almonds and water are given below. Sometimes the original instructions are to make it 'chargeaunt', or stiff, and sometimes 'rynning'. Sometimes it was made with wine or broth instead of water, but not, however, with milk as its name suggests.

Saffron, pine kernels, garlic, cardamoms, and verjuice are some of the more exotic flavourings used in medieval cookery.

Verjuice was a sharp brew of crab-apples or sour grapes and used in cooking as we use lemon juice, which is a very good substitute for verjuice. In order to preserve the verjuice during the many months between the crab-apple season and the appearance of unripe grapes, it is very probable that it was fermented. If you wish it is quite easy to make a very 'dry' wine from crab-apples that can be stored and used as required.

The recipes in this chapter are medieval to page 76, and from then on come from the eighteenth and nineteenth centuries. The differences between the two styles of cooking is readily apparent.

ALMOND MILK

4 oz (115 g) ground almonds　　　　*½ pint (284 ml) water*

Tie the almonds loosely in a piece of muslin. Pour the cold water into a basin and soak the almonds in this for several hours, occasionally shaking and squeezing the muslin until all the white 'milk' has been extracted.

To make a thicker milk, the almonds may be gently simmered in water for 10 minutes and then pressed through a food mill to make a purée.

CRUSTARDES OF EERBIS ON FYSSH DAY
FISH WITH WALNUTS AND HERBS IN PASTRY

The marvellous thing about this recipe is that by baking quite ordinary fish in the pastry case, a firm texture and crisp flavour results in something very like shellfish. Halfway through the cooking time 'the sewe', or sauce is added and this mixture of herbs and walnuts puts the finishing touch to a fish dish that can stand alone as the main course, or make a perfect supper dish. The original recipe used verjuice, that medieval brew of sour green grapes or crab-apples, with 'as mych wat' (water). But lemon juice is a good substitute. Use what herbs you have to hand and to your taste: 'gode Eerbs' are all that are specified. The meaning of the strange title is a tart of herbs on a fish, or fasting day, a day when it was forbidden to eat meat, as in Lent.

Serves 4

6 oz (170 g) shortcrust pastry
2 lbs (1 kg) fresh haddock fillets
salt and freshly milled black pepper
pinch ground cinnamon
2 tablespoons (30 ml) olive oil

For the sauce
4 oz (115 g) shelled walnuts
bunch fresh parsley
2 sprigs fresh thyme
2 sprigs fresh lemon balm
1 small sprig fresh rosemary
juice of 1 lemon and the same quantity of water
generous pinch of saffron

Roll out the pastry and line an 8-9 in (20-23 cm) pie plate and set aside. Using a sharp knife, skin the fish and chop the flesh into rough pieces. Fill the pastry case with the fish and season well with salt and pepper and a pinch of cinnamon. Spoon over the oil. Place in the centre of a moderate oven (180°C, 350°F, Gas 4) and bake for 20 minutes.

Meanwhile, prepare the sauce. Chop the walnuts coarsely, wash and strip the herbs from their stalks and chop finely or pass through a parsley mill and place in a saucepan with the walnuts. Add the lemon juice, water and saffron. Season with pepper. Simmer the ingredients all together for 5 minutes, then remove from the heat.

Spoon the sauce mixture over the top of the partly baked fish. Return to the oven and bake for a further 10 minutes. Serve hot.

ALOWS DE BEEF OR DE MOTOUN
STUFFED STEAKS IN A PIQUANT SAUCE

This dish was possibly the origin of beef olives. The stuffing is smooth in texture, slightly spicy and very green from the chopped parsley. The original recipe says 'putte hem on a round spete and roste hem till they ben y-naw'. With an oven-spit you can do this, otherwise they can be laid in a greased or oiled roasting tin and baked.

Serves 4

4 thin slices topside beef
2 medium onions
½ oz (15 g) lard
4 hard-boiled egg yolks
2 oz (55 g) fresh suet
a bunch of fresh parsley
1 heaped teaspoon (6.25 ml) saffron strands, soaked in 2 tablespoons (30 ml) hot water
or 1 level teaspoon (5 ml) powdered saffron
1 level teaspoon (5 ml) ground ginger
½ level teaspoon (2.5 ml) salt

For the sauce
2 hard-boiled egg yolks
juice of ½ lemon
4 tablespoons (60 ml) wine vinegar
½ level teaspoon (2.5 ml) ground ginger
½ level teaspoon (2.5 ml) ground cinnamon
¼ level teaspoon (1.25 ml) freshly milled pepper

Beat out the steaks to flatten them. Set aside while preparing the stuffing. Peel and finely chop the onions and fry in the lard for a few minutes until tender but not brown. Finely chop the hard-boiled egg yolks and grate the suet. Wash and finely chop the parsley. Combine the onion, chopped egg yolks, suet and parsley together in a bowl. Add the infused saffron and ginger and mix thoroughly together.

Divide the mixture equally into 4 and spread on each of the steaks. Season with salt and roll up neatly. Secure with fine string or a cocktail stick and place in an oiled or greased roasting tin. Set in a very moderate oven (170°C, 325°F, Gas 3) and bake for 30 minutes or until the steaks are done.

Meanwhile, prepare the sauce. Using a wooden spoon, cream the egg yolks with the lemon juice in a basin. Stir in the vinegar, ginger, cinnamon and pepper. Heat the mixture through gently in a small saucepan. Taste, and if the flavour is a little too sharp for your liking, add a teaspoon of sugar and the two hard-boiled egg whites, finely chopped.

Dish the steaks onto hot plates. Spoon a little of the piquant sauce on the side of each plate, or pour into a serving jug and hand separately. The recipe below would make an excellent complement to the steaks.

MAKKE

BEAN PURÉE WITH FRIED ONIONS AND WINE

Potatoes, which were introduced from the New World, were unknown in medieval England, so any floury or starchy vegetable made a good accompaniment to other dishes. A pureé made with dried beans in winter or broad beans in summer with the addition of a little wine, is nicer than mashed potato. This old recipe tells us to 'take oynons and mince hem smale seeth hem in oile til they be al bron and flourish the dissh therewith'. This is an appetizing and visual enhancement to the beans. 'Flourishing' a dish meant decorating it.

Serves 4

8 oz (225 g) dried butter beans, soaked overnight (or in summer, use 1 lb (455 g) shelled broad beans)
2 large onions

2 tablespoons (30 ml) oil
1-2 tablespoons (15-30 ml) red wine
salt to taste

Drain the beans and put in a pan with plenty of cold unsalted water. Bring to the boil, cover and simmer for about 1 hour or until the beans are soft. Drain well and beat to a pureé.

Peel and chop the onions finely. Heat the oil in a frying pan, add the onions and cook gently until they are tender and brown. Warm the wine and pour it over the bean pureé, stir and season to taste. Top with the browned onions and serve.

BEEF Y-STYWD
BEEF STEW WITH FRESH HERBS AND SPICES

The original instructions suggest that the meat should be washed and the water strained to use as part of the liquid for the first stage of cooking. Unfortunately, or perhaps fortunately, meat from a modern butcher does not have the interesting accretions which would make this operation worthwhile!

Serves 4

3½ lb (1½ kg) fore-rib of beef, on the bone
1 pint (568 ml) water
1 heaped teaspoon (6.25 ml) ground cinnamon
2 whole cardamom seeds, peeled and crushed
2 whole cloves
2 blades mace
2 large onions, finely chopped

1 tablespoon (15 ml) chopped fresh parsley
1 teaspoon (5 ml) chopped fresh sage
2 level teaspoons (10 ml) salt
4 tablespoons (60 ml) fresh breadcrumbs
1 tablespoon (15 ml) wine vinegar
large pinch saffron strands, soaked in 2 tablespoons (30 ml) hot water

Cut the meat off the bone and trim away any excess fat. Dice the flesh and place in a saucepan. Add the water and the meat bone, which gives flavour to the broth. Bring to the boil, skim and allow to simmer for 30 minutes. Remove the bone. Add the cinnamon, cardamoms, cloves, mace, onions, parsley, sage and salt. Cover the pan and allow to simmer for a further 45 minutes.

Put the breadcrumbs in a bowl and add about ⅓ pint (189 ml) – approximately – of the hot broth taken from the pan of beef. Add the vinegar and strain the mixture into a second bowl. Leave to stand for 10 minutes.

Add the infused saffron to the beef and then the breadcrumb mixture. Taste and add more salt or vinegar as required. Allow to cook for a further 45 minutes – the stew should have about 2 hours cooking time in all.

MONCHELET
SPICY LAMB IN AN AROMATIC GOLDEN SAUCE

The old instructions for this aromatic and spicy lamb stew were to 'Caste thereto erbes yhewe, gode wyne and a qntite of oynons mynced, powder fort and saffron and alye (allay) it with ayrens (eggs) and Verjuice'. 'Powder fort' was probably ginger and pepper and any of the stronger-flavoured spices, as opposed to 'powder douce' which would have combined milder flavours like cinnamon and cardamoms. The individual herbs were not specified, the choice was left to the cook and what was available in the garden and the exact quantities were always omitted from these early recipes.

Serves 4

2 lb (¾ kg) middle neck of lamb, cut in pieces
1 pint (568 ml) stock
2 heaped tablespoons (35 ml) fresh mint, chopped
1 teaspoon (5 ml) fresh thyme
1 sprig fresh marjoram
4 small or 2 large onions, peeled and chopped
½ pint (284 ml) dry white wine

pinch of saffron
pinch ground ginger
¼ level teaspoon (1.25 ml) ground cinnamon
salt and freshly milled black pepper
2 egg yolks
1 tablespoon (15 ml) lemon juice

Trim away any surplus fat and put the pieces of meat in a large saucepan. Add the stock, with the mint, thyme and marjoram, the onions and wine. Then add the saffron, ginger and cinnamon with a seasoning of salt and pepper. Cover and simmer gently for 1½ hours. Lift the meat out of the pan and keep warm in a deep serving dish.

Blend the egg yolks with a little of the hot broth taken from the pan. Return the mixture to the pan and stir over a gentle heat until it thickens (do not boil). Remove from the heat and stir in the lemon juice to sharpen the flavour. Pour over the meat and serve at once.

BURSEWS
SPICY PORK RISSOLES

These small pork rissoles are very filling and rich, so allow only 4-5 per person. Pounding the pork by hand is hard work, but that is how it would have been done in the Middle Ages with a large pestle and mortar and, perhaps, a relay of servants or helpers when the muscles began to ache. A mincer can be used, but take care not to blend the ingredients too finely – the texture should be that of a coarse pâté. Any cold leftover cooked pork is ideal for this recipe.

Serves 4

½ lb (225 g) cold cooked pork
2 hard boiled eggs
1 teaspoon (5 ml) ground coriander
¼ level teaspoon (1.25 ml) ground nutmeg
1 level teaspoon (5 ml) salt
¼ level teaspoon (1.25) freshly milled black pepper
½ teaspoon (2.5 ml) ground cinnamon

1 level teaspoon (5 ml) ground mace
2 whole cloves, crushed
½ level teaspoon (2.5 ml) caraway seeds, crushed
3 tablespoons (45 ml) flour
1 egg, beaten
1 oz (30 g) pork dripping, or lard

Finely chop or mince the pork. Mash the hard-boiled egg yolks and add to the pork together with the coriander, nutmeg, salt, pepper, cinnamon, mace, cloves and caraway seeds. Pound or mash the mixture until it becomes a fairly smooth paste.

Shape heaped teaspoons (6.25 ml spoons) of the mixture into small balls and roll each one first in flour and then in the lightly mixed egg to coat all over. From this mixture you should get about 20 little rissoles.

Heat the fat in a fairly large frying-pan, add the pork rissoles and fry gently for about 5 minutes, turning frequently until they are brown on all sides.

MORTREWYS DE FLEYSSH
SPICY MINCED PORK COOKED IN ALE

This pork dish results in a rich and subtly flavoured hash. A recipe that could be served as a main course, or as a starter with hot toast. In medieval times it would have been eaten with a spoon, or with the fingers (if cool enough!) as forks were not yet in general use. A 'trencher' or plate consisting of a large, square piece of bread would have made a good receptacle for this dish.

Serves 4

2 lb (¾ kg) spare rib of pork
1 pint (568 ml) pale ale
1 pint (568 ml) water
4 tablespoons (60 ml) fresh breadcrumbs
pinch saffron strands soaked in 2

tablespoons of hot water
salt to taste
2 egg yolks
generous pinch ground ginger

Put the pork in a large saucepan with the ale and the water. Bring to the boil and skim. Cover the pan and allow to simmer for 2 hours. Lift out the pork, remove the skin and any small bones. Reserve the cooking broth.

Finely chop or mince the cooked pork and put it in a clean saucepan. Put the breadcrumbs in a bowl and add ¼ pint (142 ml) of the reserved broth. Allow the crumbs to soak for a few minutes, then sieve the mixture into the pan with the meat. Add the infused saffron and stir in sufficient of the meat broth to make a soft, but not wet, mixture. Add salt to taste and place the pan over a low heat. When thoroughly heated through, but not boiling, stir in the egg yolks. Stir for a further few minutes until the mixture is thick, then draw off the heat. Serve hot with a generous sprinkling of ground ginger on top.

CAPOUN OR GOS FARCED
CHICKEN STUFFED WITH SPICY PORK AND GRAPES

Although the original recipe is for capon or goose, the size of either bird is extravagantly large to stuff with grapes, even though it does say 'for defawte of grapis, oynons fyrst wil y boylid and alle to-chopped' may be used. The tender whole grapes with their seasonings make a wonderful stuffing for any roast chicken. Onions as a substitute would not be nearly so unusual.

Serves 6

1 chicken about 4-4½ lb (1¾-2 kg)

For the stuffing
½ lb (225 g) lean boned pork
4 whole cloves
3 hard-boiled egg yolks
¼ lb (115 g) fresh suet
2 heaped tablespoons (35 ml) chopped fresh parsley
1 level teaspoon (5 ml) powdered saffron

dripping for roasting
½ level teaspoon (2.5 ml) ground ginger
½ level teaspoon (2.5 ml) ground cinnamon
½ level teaspoon (2.5 ml) salt
¼ level teaspoon (1.25 ml) pepper
½ lb (225 g) seedless green grapes, or halved de-seeded grapes

Wipe the chicken and set aside while preparing the stuffing. Parboil the pork for about 15 minutes, then drain and leave until cool enough to handle. Cut in pieces and pass through the mincer with the cloves. Using a wooden spoon, cream the hard-boiled egg yolks and then add the grated suet, chopped parsley, saffron, ginger, cinnamon and salt and pepper. Blend the two mixtures well and then add the whole grapes.

Use this mixture to stuff the chicken. Secure the tail skin with a skewer or cocktail sticks. Place in a roasting tin with some dripping and cover with well-greased kitchen foil. Set in the centre of a moderately hot oven (190°C, 375°F, Gas 5) and roast for 1 hour 40 minutes. Remove the foil towards the end of the cooking time to allow the breast to brown.

EGURDOUCE
RABBIT WITH RED WINE AND RAISINS, ONIONS AND SPICE

This old recipe calls for 'conyng' (rabbit) 'or kydde'. Although rabbit is more easily obtainable these days, it would make an excellent dish with kid. The meat is well browned and then topped with plump raisins and lots of fried onion before simmering in spices and red wine: a recipe that turns a rather dull rabbit into a rich and aromatic stew.

Serves 4

1 rabbit, jointed, or pieces of rabbit about 2 lb (¾ kg)
2 oz (55 g) lard
2 oz (55 g) stoned raisins
3 medium onions
¾ pint (426 ml) red wine

1 level teaspoon (5 ml) ground ginger
1 level teaspoon (5 ml) ground cinnamon
1 level teaspoon (5 ml) salt
½ level teaspoon (2.5 ml) white pepper

Wash and dry the pieces of rabbit. For a very tender dish, cover the rabbit pieces overnight with cold salted water with a bay leaf, a blade of mace and a squeeze of lemon juice added. Drain and pat the pieces dry before using.

Heat the lard in a large frying-pan and add the rabbit pieces. Fry quickly, turning the pieces frequently until they are browned on all sides. Lift the pieces out and place in a large, heavy saucepan or casserole. Add the raisins to the hot fat remaining in the pan. Fry for a few moments until they are soft and plump, then drain them from the pan with a slotted spoon and scatter over the rabbit pieces. Peel and chop the onions, and add these to the hot fat, adding a little more lard if necessary, and fry the onions until they are tender and beginning to brown. Drain with a slotted spoon and sprinkle over the rabbit pieces in the pan.

Pour in the wine and add the ginger, cinnamon, salt and pepper. Cover and simmer gently for 1½ hours or until the rabbit is tender.

CONYNG, MAWLARD IN GELY OR IN CYVEY
RABBIT OR POULTRY IN AN AROMATIC WHITE WINE SAUCE

In the Middle Ages, breadcrumbs seem to have been used to thicken sauces and stews in the same way as we would use flour today. The Romans sometimes used crumbled pastry for the same purpose. The original of this recipe tells us to 'stepe faire brede with the same broth' (the broth in which the rabbit cooked) and proceeds to 'drawe' it through a 'straynour' with 'vinegre'. This really does work and thickens the liquid without leaving any trace of crumbs. The resulting fragrant white sauce, which is not too strong tasting, would be equally good with chicken and excellent for a boiling fowl. Either could be used in place of the rabbit in this recipe.

Serves 4

1 rabbit, jointed, or 2 lb (¾ kg) rabbit pieces
1 bay leaf
1 blade mace
juice ½ lemon
½ oz (15 g) lard
½ oz (15 g) dripping
2 large onions
generous ½ pint (285 ml) chicken stock

generous ½ pint (285 ml) dry white wine
6 whole cloves
2 blades mace
½ teaspoon (2.5 ml) ground cinnamon
salt and freshly milled black pepper
2 oz (55 g) fresh breadcrumbs
2 tablespoons (30 ml) white wine vinegar
pinch ground ginger

Put the rabbit pieces in a basin and cover with cold, salted water. Add the bay leaf, mace and a squeeze of lemon juice. Leave to soak overnight.

Drain the rabbit pieces and pat them dry. Discard the water and flavourings in the basin. Heat the lard and dripping in a large, heavy saucepan. Add the rabbit pieces to the hot fat and fry gently to brown them on all sides. Remove the pieces from the pan and keep hot. Peel and finely chop the onions and add to the hot fat remaining in the pan. Fry gently for a few minutes until tender and beginning to brown. Then return the pieces of rabbit and add the stock and wine. Together they should be sufficient to cover the rabbit pieces. Add the cloves, mace, cinnamon and a seasoning of salt and plenty of pepper. Cover and simmer gently for 1 hour.

Put the breadcrumbs in a bowl and mix about ⅓ pint (189 ml) of the hot broth from the rabbit. Pass through a sieve into a small saucepan. Bring to the boil and then return the mixture to the pan with the rabbit, adding a pinch of ginger. Cover the pan again and allow to cook gently for a further 30 minutes. Check the seasoning and serve, possibly with the dish below.

SPYNOCHES YFRYED
SPINACH WITH NUTMEG AND OLIVE OIL

A medieval way of cooking spinach which is beautifully simple and subtle in flavour. After cooking, the spinach is turned in olive oil and enlivened with a little nutmeg. Butter, which we would add to spinach, was too precious to be used in cooking; the 'dairy' cows of those days produced scarcely more milk than would feed a calf; but you will find that the olive oil marries with spinach even more harmoniously.

Serves 4

2 lb (1 kg) fresh spinach   little grated nutmeg
2 tablespoons (30 ml) olive oil

Wash the spinach and tear out the mid-ribs, drain and add the damp leaves to a large saucepan. Cover and cook for 5-10 minutes or until the spinach is quite tender. Drain the spinach well and press in a colander to remove all excess liquid.

Turn on to a board and roughly chop into squares with a knife. Return to a clean pan with the olive oil and a little grated nutmeg. Reheat gently, turning the spinach with a wooden spoon until it is well coated all over.

PEIONS YSTEWED
STUFFED PIGEONS COOKED IN A CASSEROLE WITH VERJUICE AND SPICES

Here is an opportunity to serve a truly medieval meal. The pigeons should be served whole, one per person, on a plate or trencher of bread. They should be eaten with the fingers, so provide large finger bowls and plenty of napkins.

Serves 4

4 pigeons
12 large whole cloves of garlic
2 teaspoons (10 ml) chopped fresh thyme
2 teaspoons (10 ml) chopped fresh marjoram
2 teaspoons (10 ml) chopped fresh sage
2 tablespoons (30 ml) chopped fresh parsley
½ pint (284 ml) light stock

3 tablespoons (45 ml) verjuice, or the juice of ½ lemon
pinch of saffron strands
½ level teaspoon (2.5 ml) ground cinnamon
¼ level teaspoon (1.25 ml) ground ginger
½ oz (15 g) lard

The pigeons should be plucked, drawn and ready for roasting. Remove any papery outer coating from the cloves of garlic. Divide the garlic and herbs equally into 4 portions and stuff the inside of each pigeon with the mixture.

Put the pigeons in a casserole which is just big enough to take them. Pour over the stock, add the lemon juice, the saffron, cinnamon and ginger and finally the lard. Cover with a lid, put in the centre of a moderate oven (180°C, 350°F, Gas 4) and cook for 1½ hours or until very tender. It is especially important that the pigeons should be really tender if you are going to eat them by hand. They should be almost falling apart: if necessary allow an extra 15 minutes' cooking time to ensure this.

FRUTOURS
APPLE FRITTERS IN A BATTER MADE WITH ALE

These slim, tender apple fritters are coated in the lightest of batters, made with yeast and ale – the taste of the ale is just discernible. Follow the original instructions and having peeled and cored the apples 'cut hem thyn like obleies' (communion wafers). Four large cooking apples make a lot of fritters, but they melt in the mouth and will disappear fast.

Serves 4

4 large cooking apples

For the batter
4 oz (115 g) plain flour
pinch salt
½ oz (15 g) fresh yeast
3 tablespoons (45 ml) warm water
½ level teaspoons (2.5 ml) sugar
6 tablespoons (90 ml) pale ale
2 egg yolks
2-3 oz (55-85 g) lard for frying

Sift the flour and salt into a bowl. Blend the yeast with the warm water and add the sugar. Pour into the centre of the flour. Add the pale ale, and using a wooden spoon draw in the flour and beat well to make a smooth batter. Cover with a cloth and leave in a warm place for 30 minutes. Lightly mix the egg yolks and stir into the batter before using.

Peel, core and slice the apples thinly. Dip them in the batter and then add to a frying-pan of melted, hot lard. Fry until they are golden brown, turning them to cook both sides. Fry a few at a time, adding flakes of lard to the pan as needed. Serve the hot fritters dusted with caster sugar.

PEER IN CONFYT
PEARS STEWED WITH WINE AND GINGER

A particularly delicious compôte of pears first stewed in red wine, then simmered in a syrup of white wine, sugar and ginger. The old recipe tells us to use 'wyne greke' (Greek), but any sweet white wine would do. While the pears simmer in their syrup, the kitchen is filled with the most heavenly warm, spicy smell.

Serve cold, or hot with a jug of chilled thick cream if you agree to sacrifice absolute authenticity.

Serves 4

2 lb (1 kg) cooking pears
½ pint (284 ml) red wine
½ pint (284 ml) sweet white wine

6 oz (170 g) caster sugar
1 level teaspoon ground ginger

Peel, halve and core the pears. Place the pears cut side down close together in a shallow pan with the red wine. Bring to the boil, cover and stew gently for 30 minutes or until the pears are tender. Remove the pan lid for the last 10 minutes so that the wine is well reduced. Drain the pears.

Place the white wine, sugar and ginger in a clean saucepan and bring to the boil, stirring to dissolve the sugar. Simmer for 5 minutes, then add the pears and cook for a further 5 minutes. Serve in the syrup.

RAPEYE
APPLE PUDDING WITH GROUND RICE AND SPICED WINE

The old recipe is full of typical medieval ingredients and instructions. Dessert apples were used, and we are required to 'stampe hem' to achieve a pulped consistency. The dish was coloured 'wyth safran an wyth sauderys', the latter made from sandalwood and producing a rich red colour. A drop of cochineal is permissible if you want to make the dish resplendent, but the use of red wine and saffron helps the colouring anyway. Finally, the much esteemed almond milk is included and this should be made overnight, or a few hours before starting the recipe.

Serves 4-6

4 oz (115 g) dried dates
½ pint (284 ml) almond milk (page 58)
2 lb (1 kg) dessert apples
½ pint (284 ml) red wine
½ teaspoon (2.5 ml) ground ginger
1 level teaspoon (5 ml) ground cinnamon
½ teaspoon (2.5 ml) ground mace
6 cloves, crushed
2 level tablespoons (30 ml) ground rice
pinch saffron strands, soaked in 2 tablespoons (30 ml) hot water

Stone and finely chop the dates and put them in a saucepan with the almond milk. Peel, core and chop the apples and add to the saucepan along with the wine and the ginger, cinnamon, mace and cloves. Bring to the boil, cover and simmer gently for 5 minutes. Mash the apple with a wooden or slotted spoon and continue to cook until soft and well pulped.

Stir in the ground rice and the infused saffron and cook for a further 20 minutes. Taste and add sugar if desired. The mixture should be fairly thick, or 'chargeaunt' as the old recipe describes the consistency. Serve hot with extra cinnamon sprinkled on top.

COMADORE
PASTRY FINGERS FILLED WITH SPICED MIXED FRUITS

These little fingers of pastry filled with spiced apple, pears, tender figs and raisins stewed in red wine, are not unlike mince pies. The old recipe requires that the mixture is stirred 'warliche', (warily) 'to keep it wel from brenyng' and this is a wise instruction for it quickly becomes thick and could easily stick to the pan. When cold, the mixture is cut into 'smale pecys of the greatnesse and the length of a litel fyner, closed fast in gode paste and fryed in oile'. They would make an original touch to a conventional Christmas dinner and could be kept warm or reheated in the oven. The filling can be made up in advance.

Makes 26

½ lb (225 g) dried figs (if hard, soak them overnight)
¼ lb (115 g) stoned raisins
½ pint (284 ml) red wine
1 lb (455 g) cooking apples
1 lb (455 g) pears
4 oz (115 g) caster sugar
2 tablespoons (30 ml) vegetable oil
3 cloves, crushed

½ teaspoon (2.5 ml) ground mace
½ level teaspoon (2.5 ml) cinnamon
generous pinch ground ginger
pinch salt
1 tablespoon (15 ml) flaked almonds
6 oz (170 g) shortcrust pastry (see below)
oil for frying

Wash the figs and raisins and put them in a saucepan with the wine. Bring to the boil, then simmer for 30 minutes or until tender. Drain, reserving the liquor, and purée the fruit. Meanwhile, peel and core the apples and pears and keep in cold water until needed.

Add the sugar to the reserved wine liquid. Stir over low heat until the sugar has dissolved and then bring to the boil. Strain on to the purée of fruit. Chop the apples and pears and place in the saucepan together with the fruit purée. Cover and cook the mixture gently for 30 minutes, or until the fruit is quite soft.

Put the oil in a clean saucepan. Add the cooked fruit mixture, the cloves, mace, cinnamon, ginger, salt and almonds. Cook gently, uncovered and stirring occasionally to prevent the mixture from sticking, until it is really thick. Turn out on to a flat dish, spread level and leave until quite cold.

On a floured surface, roll the pastry out thinly to an oblong.

Cut into pieces about 4 in (10 cm) long × 2½ in (6 cm) wide. Damp all edges and lay on each oblong of pastry a little of the filling 'the greatnesse and length' of a little finger. With floured fingers carefully seal the edges. Heat a little oil in a frying-pan and gently fry the comadores until golden brown, or place on an oiled baking tray, set in a moderate oven (180°C, 350°F, Gas 4) and bake for 30 minutes.

Serve on a hot plate dusted with extra caster sugar.

SHORTCRUST PASTRY

6 oz (175 g) plain flour
pinch of salt
1½ oz (37 g) butter

1½ oz (37 g) white cooking fat
3 tablespoons (45 ml) cold water

Sift the flour and salt into a mixing bowl. Using a palette knife, blend the butter and white cooking fat on a plate and add in pieces to the sifted flour. Pick up the mixture in small handfuls and rub fat into the flour with the fingertips, allowing the ingredients to fall back into the bowl between the fingers. Continue until fat is evenly blended and mixture looks like fine breadcrumbs. There should be no loose flour in the bowl.

Sprinkle the water evenly over the mixture and stir with a table knife or fork, cutting through the mixture, until the dough clings together and leaves the sides of the bowl clean. Turn on to a lightly floured surface and knead once or twice to remove the cracks. Allow dough to rest for 15-20 minutes. Bake in an oven heated to 200°C, 400°F, Gas 6 unless otherwise indicated.

SIMPLE SOUP
CREAM OF VEGETABLE SOUP

This recipe was taken from a collection of recipes for the family and for the sickroom. The author claimed that this soup 'cannot be said to contain either gout or scurvy'. Whatever its medicinal properties, it has a fresh, light flavour and is thick and satisfying: an excellent soup for the first taste of spring. The original suggested that 'some part of the vegetables may be left unpulped' to provide some solid pieces in the soup, which is an alternative you may prefer.

Serves 6

2 large carrots
3 medium white turnips
3 medium potatoes
4 pints (2¼ litres) light stock
4 sticks celery
outer leaves of an average lettuce,
excluding the heart

5-6 oz (150-170 g) curly endive
1 oz (30 g) parsley
salt and freshly milled black pepper
2 oz (55 g) butter
1 oz (30 g) flour

Peel and coarsely chop the carrots, turnips and potatoes and put them in a large saucepan with the stock. Wash and roughly chop the celery, lettuce, curly endive and parsley and add to the pan. Season with salt and pepper. Bring to the boil and simmer gently for 1 hour or until the vegetables are quite tender. Pass the vegetables and liquid from the pan through a sieve or food mill to make a purée.

Rinse out the saucepan and replace over the heat. Add the butter and when melted, stir in the flour. Cook for a few minutes, then stir in the purée and bring up to the boil. Simmer for 15 minutes. Check the seasoning and serve.

GREEN PEASE SOUP WITHOUT MEAT
THICK PEA SOUP GARNISHED BY TENDER YOUNG PEAS

The title of the old recipe suggests that because it was made 'without meat' the soup would have been served during Lent or on one of the religious fast days.

For anyone with a garden, or even those faced with the end-of-season bullets sometimes sold in shops, it is an ideal way of converting old peas into a delicious soup to which young peas, cucumber and lettuce give body and freshness. The original recipe recommended adding some spoonfuls of spinach juice to the soup if not sufficiently green, and nowadays it could be made with dried peas and frozen peas.

Serves 4-6

1 pint (568 ml) shelled old peas
2 pints (1136 ml) water
2-3 sprigs mint
2 level teaspoons (10 ml) salt
½ pint (284 ml) shelled young peas
½ cucumber

1 medium onion
handful of lettuce, with as much stalk as possible
1 oz (30 g) butter
½ level teaspoon (2.5 ml) white pepper
salt to taste

Put the old peas into a large saucepan with the water, mint and salt. Bring to the boil, cover and cook gently for about 30-35 minutes, or until the peas are soft. Remove the mint. Strain and reserve the liquor. Purée the peas through a food mill or sieve, adding a little of the hot liquor if the mixture is very thick. Return the purée to a clean saucepan and add the reserved liquor and the young peas.

Peel the cucumber and cut into cubes. Peel and chop the onion and wash and finely shred the lettuce and stalk. Add these to the pan of soup, along with the butter, pepper and salt if required. Simmer for 25 minutes until the onion is tender, then serve.

To Bake Fish Cod and Shellfish
A RICH PIE WITH SALMON AND SHRIMPS

This anything but humble fish pie is typical of the lavish use of ingredients in the nineteenth century. The spices and generous use of butter would make a well-flavoured and rich pie with any fish, but the instructions are to take 'the same quantity of salmon' as cod, and 'when shrimps cannot be had, a tail of a lobster will supply their place'. When you are feeling extravagant, you will not be disappointed in this dish.

Serves 4-6

1 lb (455 g) cooked fresh cod
1 lb (455 g) cooked fresh salmon
4 oz (115 g) peeled fresh or frozen shrimps
¼ level teaspoon (1.25 ml) ground mace
¼ level teaspoon (1.25 ml) ground cloves
1 level teaspoon (5 ml) salt
pinch cayenne pepper
1 level teaspoon (5 ml) freshly milled black pepper
4 oz (115 g) butter
1 large egg
2 oz (55 g) fresh white breadcrumbs
a little extra butter

Flake the cod and salmon into a basin and carefully remove any skin and bones. Roughly chop the shrimps, first draining off any liquid if using frozen shrimps, and add to the fish in the basin. Add the mace, cloves, salt and cayenne and black pepper. Melt the butter in a small pan and pour it over the ingredients in the basin. Lightly mix the egg and stir into the flaked fish mixture, add half the breadcrumbs and mix to bind the ingredients together.

Butter an ovenproof dish, fill with the fish mixture and spread the top level. Scatter the remaining breadcrumbs over the top and dot with some flakes of butter. Set in a moderately hot oven (190°C, 375°F, Gas 5) and bake for 30 minutes until well heated and the crumbs are crisp and brown.

TURBOT
TURBOT POACHED IN WINES WITH ANCHOVY

The original recipe recommended using a whole turbot 'which in this mode of dressing must be small', but most recipes from the eighteenth century called for huge quantities, and even a small turbot would be large for most modern families. Four nice thick steaks cut from across the fish make a good meal for four people and the beautifully rich and unusual sauce makes it worthy of a connoisseur. The use of two wines is extravagant, perhaps not essential, but decidedly delicious.

Serves 4

4 steaks of turbot, about 1½ in (3½ cm) thick
seasoned flour
lard for frying

For the sauce
¼ pint (142 ml) dry white wine
¼ pint (142 ml) red wine
3 anchovy fillets
½ level teaspoon (2.5 ml) salt
little grated nutmeg
½ teaspoon (2.5 ml) ginger
1 oz (30 g) butter
1 level tablespoon (15 ml) flour
3 slices lemon, rind and pith removed

Rinse the fish steaks, dry them thoroughly then dip into seasoned flour. Select a pan large enough to hold the turbot steaks and set over moderate heat. Melt in it sufficient lard to give ½ in (1 cm) of melted fat. When hot, gently add the floured fish steaks and fry on both sides until golden brown. Lift from the pan and drain on absorbent paper.

Put the fish in a clean pan and add the wines, the anchovy fillets, salt, nutmeg and ginger. Cover and cook very gently for 25 minutes or until the liquid is reduced by half. Blend the butter with the flour and add the pan liquid. Stir until the sauce thickens, then add the slices of lemon. Simmer for a further 5 minutes.

Lift the turbot on to a hot serving dish, the surfaces of which you have rubbed with a piece of shallot.

Pour the sauce over the fish and serve with plain boiled potatoes.

TROUT
STUFFED TROUT IN A WINE AND CREAM SAUCE

The trout are first stuffed with a soft herb and lemon-flavoured mixture, then cooked in wine and seasoning and finally served in their own rich but delicate sauce. The old recipe used parsley and 'savoury herbs'. A little marjoram, dill, tarragon or chervil could replace the thyme and rosemary. In our great grandmother's day, there were enough trout in the streams and rivers for most country folk to be able to catch enough for themselves and their families. Sadly, this lovely fish has been much depleted and wild fish are only found where landowners and clubs preserve special trout streams at great expense and let out the fishing rights for a lot of money. The fish from trout farms can in no way compare in texture and flavour to the wild ones, but if you are not among the lucky people who can catch their own trout, then this recipe will do a lot for the tired specimens on the fishmonger's slab.

Serves 4

4 trout

For the stuffing
4 oz (115 g) fresh breadcrumbs
1 oz (30) butter, softened
½ heaped tablespoon (7 ml) mixed
chopped parsley, thyme and rosemary
1 level teaspoon (5 ml) salt
freshly milled black pepper
pinch grated nutmeg
grated rind of ½ lemon
1 egg yolk

For the sauce
4 black peppercorns and 3 cloves
2 pieces finely pared lemon rind
1 onion, thinly sliced in rings
½ pint (284 ml) red wine
¼ pint (142 ml) stock
4 tablespoons (60 ml) double cream
flour
1 tablespoon (15 ml) lemon juice

Ask your fishmonger to remove the heads and gut the trout without slitting the belly. If bought already cleaned, use cocktail sticks and thread to secure the fish closed after the stuffing. Wash and thoroughly dry the trout.

Put the breadcrumbs in a bowl with the softened butter, chopped herbs, salt and pepper, nutmeg, grated lemon rind and work all together with a fork. When evenly mixed, stir in the egg yolk. Divide the mixture into four portions and use to stuff the trout.

Lay the fish neatly in a large saucepan with the peppercorns, cloves, lemon rind, onion rings, wine and stock. Bring slowly to the boil. Cover and cook gently for 20 minutes. Lift the trout on to a hot dish and keep warm. Mix the flour and cream together. Add the lemon juice and a little of the hot liquid from the pan. Stir to blend and return the mixture to the remaining pan liquid. Bring to the boil and stir until the sauce thickens. Pour the sauce over the fish and serve.

Before Columbus discovered America and before the great interchange of plants between the Old World and the New began, the only beans known in Europe were broad beans. Cooked with a sprig or two of savory, the herb traditionally used to flavour beans, they make a delicious vegetable to serve with trout, and in early summer when beans are young and tender, the wild brown trout are in season. Our ancestors were blissfully ignorant of trout farms and frozen beans, so, for a truly authentic meal, go to the river for your fish and the garden for your herbs and beans.

Serves 4

4 lb (2 kg) fresh young broad beans   2 oz (55 g) butter
2 or 3 sprigs savory

Shell the beans and plunge into a small amount of boiling unsalted water, add the savory, cover and cook for 7 minutes, or until the beans are just tender. Drain and remove the savory. Return the beans to the pan in which you have melted the butter. Shake and swirl until the beans are glistening. Serve in a hot dish.

BEEF WITH CUCUMBER
STEAKS WITH CUCUMBER AND ONION SAUCE

You will get the best results with this dish if you have a really well-flavoured stock in which to cook the vegetables. The brown jelly from beneath a bowl of dripping or a mixture of leftover brown gravy that was made with pan juices from a roast joint, plus an equal quantity of good quality beef stock give a good, rich, brown sauce. Cucumbers were widely grown both in cottage gardens and in the greenhouses of big country houses, the use of two whole cucumbers in this dish is a measure of their popularity. It should be served at once to retain the delicate succulence of the cucumber.

Serves 4

4 pieces of rump steak
salt and freshly milled black pepper
2 medium onions
2 cucumbers

5 oz (140 g) butter
1 heaped tablespoon (17.25 ml) flour
½ pint (284 ml) good beef stock

Beat the steaks to flatten them and season with salt and pepper. Peel and thinly slice the onions. Peel the cucumbers, cut in four lengthwise and remove the seeds. Cut the cucumber flesh into 1-in (2½-cm) long sticks.

Melt 3 oz (85 g) of the butter in a large saucepan. Add the onions and fry gently until tender and brown. Add the cucumber, cover with a lid and cook gently for 5 minutes. Remove the lid and simmer for a further 10 minutes. Season well with salt and pepper and stir in the flour. Gradually add the stock, stirring all the time until the sauce has thickened. Cover and simmer for 10 minutes, or until cucumber is quite tender.

Melt the remaining 2 oz (55 g) butter in a large frying pan. Add the steaks and fry quickly on either side until well browned, then lower the heat and cook according to your taste. Lift the steaks from the pan on to a hot dish. Pour over the cucumber and onion sauce and serve.

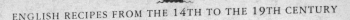

To Fry Beef Steaks
STEAKS COOKED IN ALE WITH ONION AND HERBS

The brown ale in this recipe gives a rich gravy and a fine flavour to the steaks, which should not be ragged as in a stew, but whole and tender. Ale would have been brewed with hops by this time, although it was still rejected in Queen Elizabeth's reign when an edict was issued against the use of 'that pernicious weed, the hop.' But by the eighteenth century hops were accepted and the beer we use for this recipe will not be far different from the original brew.

Serves 4

4 pieces rump steak, about 4 oz (115 g) each
½ pint (284 ml) brown ale
1 large onion
2-3 sprigs thyme
small bunch fresh parsley

½ level teaspoon (2.5 ml) salt
freshly milled black pepper
little grated nutmeg
½ oz (15 g) butter
½ tablespoon (2.5 ml) flour

Trim and beat the steaks well with a rolling-pin to flatten. Put them in a large pan with the ale, bring to the boil slowly, then cover and cook for 10 minutes.

Slice the onion thinly. Wash and strip the herbs from their stalks and chop them finely. Add the herbs and onion to the steaks with the salt, pepper and nutmeg. Work the butter and flour together, add to the pan and shake or stir to blend. Recover and cook gently for a further 45 minutes to 1 hour, or until the steaks are tender and the gravy is thick and well flavoured.

HAUNCH OF VENISON
VENISON IN A RICH CAPER SAUCE

The Duke of Bolton's cook served venison in this way in 1734 so that, though well done, it is exceptionally juicy and moist. The marinade in which the meat has lain is used to baste the joint during roasting. A caper sauce is served with the venison and is enriched with a 'cullis'. This was a special stock sometimes using quantities of veal, lean ham and chicken as well as vegetables, and was used solely to enrich sauces, stews or 'ragoos' as they were described. I give instructions for larding the joint which is part of the original recipe's excellence, but if you don't possess a larding needle, you may lay some rashers of fat bacon over the joint as it roasts.

Serves 6-8

haunch of venison, weighing about 4 lb (1¼ kg)

For the marinade
1 pint (568 ml) white wine
juice of 1 lemon
2 level teaspoons (10 ml) salt
2-3 parsley stalks
2-4 sprigs thyme
2-3 sage leaves
1 sprig rosemary
4 bay leaves
3 slices lemon

For larding
2 rashers streaky bacon
1 level teaspoon salt
½ level teaspoon (2.5 ml) freshly milled black pepper
½ level teaspoon (2.5 ml) crushed cloves
½ level teaspoon (2.5 ml) grated nutmeg

For the sauce
1 oz (30 g) butter
the cullis (see below)
2 heaped tablespoons (12.5 ml) capers
juice of ½ lemon
freshly milled black pepper and salt to taste

Wipe the venison. Cut the bacon rashers into strips or 'lardons' about ¼ in thick (½ cm wide × 2 in (5 cm) long. Mix the salt, pepper, cloves and nutmeg together and roll the 'lardons' in the seasoning. With a larding needle 'sew' each strip into the meat at intervals of about an inch (2½ cm).

Measure the wine, lemon juice and salt into a deep dish. Add the parsley stalks, thyme, sage, rosemary, bay leaves and lemon slices. Lay the larded venison in this and leave to marinate for 3-4 hours or overnight, turning the meat occasionally during this time.

Heat the butter in a self-basting roasting tin. Drain the venison from the marinade and place in the hot butter. Strain the marinade and add a few spoonfuls to the meat in the pan. Cover with the lid and set in a slow oven (170°C, 325°F, Gas 3) and roast for 3 hours. Baste with the rest of the marinade during the cooking time until it is all used up.

When the venison is tender and well cooked, dish and keep hot. Pour off the surplus fat from the pan. Put the 'cullis' and pan drippings that remain in a small saucepan and boil up. Continue to cook, uncovered, until the mixture is reduced to a strong gravy. Stir in the capers and lemon juice. Check the seasoning and add pepper and salt if needed.

Serve in a hot sauce-boat with the venison.

A FAMILY CULLIS
A STRONG STOCK TO ENRICH SAUCES

A simple version of 'a family cullis' can be made in advance, cooled and strained ready to use.

1 oz (30 g) butter, rolled in flour
½ pint (284 ml) stock
2-3 oz (55-85 g) mushrooms
3 tablespoons (45 ml) good gravy (left over from a joint or from brown jelly underneath the dripping)
1 glass white wine

bunch parsley, thyme and basil tied together
1 bay leaf
2 cloves
2 blades mace
½ level teaspoon (2.5 ml) salt
plenty of freshly milled black pepper

Melt the butter and flour in a saucepan. Add the stock slowly and stir to blend. Wash and slice the mushrooms and add them to the pan along with the gravy, wine, bunch of herbs, bay leaf, cloves, mace, salt and pepper. Bring to the boil, cover and cook gently for 1 hour. Cool, skim off the fat and strain through a fine strainer and use to make the sauce in the preceding recipe.

To Make French Cutlets, Very Good
CHOPS STUFFED WITH ANCHOVIES AND HERBS

'Then butter as many pieces of white Paper as you have cutlets, and wrap them up every one by themselves, turn up the edges of the Papers with great care that none of the moisture gets out; therefore let the Papers be large enough to turn up several times at the edge; and if occasion be, stick a pin to keep it all in; for this Gravy is all their Sauce.'

This detailed description suggests that it was a new idea. The use of paper was probably a natural development from the crusts of flour and water that were used earlier to protect all cuts of meat and poultry during cooking. Nowadays, foil is an easy substitute.

Serves 8

8 lamb chump chops

For the stuffing
½ lb (225 g) lean leg of pork, finely minced
½ lb (225 g) fresh white breadcrumbs
¼ lb (115 g) shredded beef suet
4 anchovy fillets pounded with a small knob of butter
1 heaped teaspoon (6.25 ml) chopped

fresh thyme, or ½ teaspoon (2.5 ml) dried
1 tablespoon (15 ml) chopped parsley
1 teaspoon (5 ml) chopped fresh marjoram, or ½ teaspoon (2.5 ml) dried
salt and freshly milled black pepper to taste
1 level teaspoon (5 ml) grated nutmeg
2 onions, finely chopped
3 egg yolks

Using a small sharp knife, trim the chops neatly and pull any skin away from the fat. Cut from the fatty side through the meat towards the bone until each chop is almost halved horizontally.

Put all the ingredients for the stuffing into a large bowl, adding the egg yolks last. Stir to mix, and then knead well to bind the ingredients together. Divide the mixture into 8 portions, then halve each one. Without using flour, shape each portion into a roll the size of a small sausage. Flatten slightly and place one piece inside, and one on top of each chop.

Cut 8 pieces of foil 12 in (30 cm) square and butter them well. Wrap each chop individually, folding the foil edge tightly but allowing space for swelling. Arrange in a shallow roasting tin and place in a moderately hot oven (190°C, 375°F, Gas 5) for 30-40 minutes.

Unwrap the foil and serve the chops in their own juice.

To Stew a Hare
TENDER HARE WITH ANCHOVIES, HERBS AND CLARET

The long gentle cooking reduces the hare in this recipe to a very tender stew. The old recipe recommends 'stewing leisurely' for 6-7 hours, then to 'take out what bones you can find, with the herbs and onion, if not dissolved'. However, 2½-3 hours is quite enough to tenderize the meat, if not to dissolve the herbs and onion! The final instructions 'you need only shake it up with half a poind of butter when ready for the table' illustrates the lavishness of eighteenth-century cooking. A knob of butter is enough, but the claret recommended does greatly enhance the flavour of the gravy.

Serves 4

2 lb (¾ kg) hare pieces
small bunch of parsley
2-3 sprigs thyme, marjoram and sage
1 large onion, finely chopped
1½ level teaspoons (7.5 ml) salt

freshly milled black pepper
1½ pints (¾ litre) strong stock
1 pint (568 ml) claret
2 anchovy fillets
2 oz (55 g) butter

Trim and wash the hare pieces. Dry thoroughly and put in a large saucepan with the fresh herbs tied in a bundle. Add onion, salt, pepper and stock. Bring slowly to the boil, cover and simmer for 1½ hours.

Add the claret and the anchovies pounded with 1 oz (30 g) of the butter. Recover and cook gently for a further hour. Lift out the herbs and any loose bones. Stir in the remaining butter and serve hot.

TO FRICASSEY CHICKENS OR SWEETBREADS
CHICKEN COOKED IN WINE WITH A LEMONY CREAM SAUCE

It is important to follow the instructions of the original recipe which said 'set them on in as much water as will cover them; when they boil up scum them very clean, then take them out and strain the liquor'; this would have been particularly important if using sweetbreads instead of chicken, but in either case it makes a great deal of difference to the delicacy of the final sauce, which has a beautiful texture and taste. If using sweetbreads, soak them first for a couple of hours in several changes of cold water, then pull away any fat and surplus skin before following the recipe for chicken.

Serves 6

4½ lb (2 kg) roasting chicken
water
4 black peppercorns
salt and freshly milled black pepper
1 blade mace
finely pared rind of ½ lemon
1 small onion, stuck with 4 cloves
¼ pint (142 ml) dry white wine

For the sauce
1 level tablespoon (15 ml) plain flour
3 tablespoons (45 ml) cream
1 egg yolk
little grated nutmeg
juice of ½ lemon
½ oz (15 g) butter

Joint the chicken, skin and wash the pieces and put in a large saucepan with enough cold water to cover. Bring to the boil and carefully skim the surface. Take out the chicken pieces, strain the liquid and reserve about ½ pint (284 ml) for further cooking. Return the chicken pieces to the clean saucepan and add the reserved liquid. Add the whole peppercorns, a seasoning of salt and pepper, the mace, lemon rind and onion stuck with cloves. Cover with a lid and bring to the boil. Warm the wine and add to the pan. Allow the chicken to simmer for 1½ hours, or until tender. Remove the pan from the heat and discard the onion.

Blend the flour, cream and egg yolk in a small bowl until smooth and add a little grated nutmeg. Add about 6-8 tablespoons (90-120 ml) of the hot chicken liquid and blend well. Gradually stir this mixture into the saucepan containing the chicken. Stir constantly as the sauce thickens and bring just to a simmer (do not boil). Cook gently for 2-3 minutes, then add the lemon juice and butter. Stir to blend and serve.

A WHIPT SILLIBUB, EXTRAORDINARY
CREAM WITH LEMON AND WHITE WINE

The earliest syllabubs were made by milking a cow straight into a bowl containing some ale or cider. This was allowed to stand until a curd formed on the top of the ale-flavoured whey, which posed a practical problem, for the dish had to be partly eaten, partly drunk. Later on, wine was used in place of ale, and cream instead of milk. By the eighteenth century, the proportion of cream was increased and the wine reduced until the final mixture was uniformly thick and of a delicious lightness and delicacy of flavour. It was then written of as 'an everlasting Syllabub'.

Serves 6

thinly pared rind and juice of 1 lemon
¼ pint (142 ml) white wine

2 oz (55 g) caster sugar
generous ½ pint (284 ml) double cream

Soak the pared lemon rind in the wine for 2-3 hours before starting the recipe.

Squeeze the lemon and strain the wine and lemon juice into a deep bowl. Add the sugar and stir well until dissolved. Slowly stir in the cream, then whisk with a hand or rotary whisk until the mixture thickens to a soft peak.

Spoon into glasses and stand in a cool place until next day. Choose a cool larder in preference to a refrigerator. This syllabub will keep for 2 or 3 days and is an insubstantial but rich dessert.

PANCAKES, CALL'D A QUIRE OF PAPER
RICHLY FLAVOURED PANCAKES MADE WITH CREAM

These pancakes are the nearest in truth to the old 'melt in the mouth' description that you will ever come across. They are so rich, but thin and melting that their exquisite texture entirely justifies the wild extravagance of the ingredients: they would have provided a satisfying touch of luxury on Shrove Tuesday before the dull menus of Lent descended on most households.

Serves 4

4 oz (115 g) butter
½ pint (284 ml) double cream
3 eggs
2 tablespoons (30 ml) plain flour

1 tablespoon (15 ml) sherry
1 teaspoon (5 ml) orange flower water
½ tablespoon (7 ml) caster sugar
little grated nutmeg, optional

Melt the butter in a small pan, remove from the heat and allow to cool. Put the cream in a large mixing basin. Break in the eggs and mix together with a fork. Sift the flour and add to the cream and egg mixture, beating well to make a smooth batter. Stir in the sherry, the orange flower water and the sugar and last of all the melted butter. Add a little nutmeg, if liked.

Heat a small frying-pan and grease it with butter for the first pancake only. Pour in just enough batter to cover the pan very thinly and tilt the pan to spread the batter over the base. Cook one side, then flip the pancake over with a fish-slice or palette knife and fry the other side until speckly brown. Slide on to a hot plate and dust with caster sugar. Stack the pancakes, sprinkling each one with sugar and keep warm until they are all cooked.

THE BEST ORANGE PUDDING THAT EVER WAS TASTED
CREAMY ORANGE-FLAVOURED CURD PIE

The rather fulsome title is hardly an exaggeration, this really is a mouth-watering sweet. The pastry case is filled with a luscious orange-flavoured amber jelly, rather like orange curd. The original recipe used Seville oranges and their bitter-sweet taste is very subtle. But the grated rind of a lemon and a large sweet orange should be nice enough when Seville oranges are out of season.

Serves 4

6 oz (170 g) shortcrust pastry (page 75)

For the filling
4 oz (115 g) butter
4 oz (115 g) caster sugar
6 egg yolks
grated rind of 2 Seville oranges or the grated rind of 1 lemon and 1 large sweet orange

Roll out the pastry and use to line an 8-in (20-cm) buttered pie plate. Line with a square of greaseproof paper filled with a layer of rice, or with a piece of crumpled kitchen foil, to hold down the base of the pastry. Set in a moderately hot oven (190°C, 375°F, Gas 5) and bake 'blind' for 20 minutes. Remove the piece of greaseproof paper and rice, or foil, a few minutes before the end of the baking time.

Cream the butter, sugar and grated orange rind together. Beat in the egg yolks one at a time. When the mixture is smooth and creamy pour into the pastry shell. Set in a slow oven (150°C, 300°F, Gas 2) and bake for 45 minutes, or until the mixture is set and the top golden. If the top becomes brown a little too quickly, cover with a piece of foil after the first 20 minutes. Serve hot or cold.

FOR TO MAKE TARTYS IN APPLIS
SPICY APPLE TART WITH RAISINS AND FIGS

There are several descriptions of different types of pastry given in the medieval recipes and 'tartys' are generally referred to as 'fayre paste', which suggests that the pastry was eaten, as in this recipe, and not just used as a container. It is an example of dried fruits and apples being used to give a taste of freshness and variety to the winter diet, with spices and saffron to add an exotic flavour. Saffron was much used in the Middle Ages for flavouring and colouring. It was widely grown and therefore relatively less expensive than it is today.

Serve 4-6

2 lb (¾ kg) dessert apples
1 lb (½ kg) pears
2 oz (55 g) stoned raisins, chopped
1 or 2 chopped dried figs
1 level teaspoon (5 ml) cinnamon

1 pinch ground nutmeg
2 tablespoons (30 ml) water
pinch of saffron strands
4 oz (115 g) shortcrust pastry

Peel, core and cut up the apples and pears. Place in a good-sized saucepan along with the chopped raisins and figs, the cinnamon and nutmeg. Add the water. Cover the pan with a lid and cook very gently, shaking the pan occasionally, until the mixture is well pulped and reduced. Flavour with a pinch of saffron.

Line an 8-in (20-cm) flan ring with the shortcrust pastry. Pour in the hot apple mixture and spread level. Place above centre in a hot oven (200°C, 400°F, Gas 6) and bake for 35 or 40 minutes. Serve warm or cold.

TO STEW GOLDEN PIPPINS A VERY GOOD WAY
APPLES COOKED IN SUGAR AND LEMON

Any yellow dessert apple can be used that will cook tender and clear-looking and hold its shape. 'Double-refin'd Sugar' was used in this and many of the eighteenth-century recipes. The sugar sold would have been coarse and dirty and would have needed further grinding and sifting.

Serves 4

1 pint (568 ml) water
½ lb (225 g) caster sugar
6 Golden Delicious apples

juice of ½ lemon
2-3 pieces finely pared lemon rind

Put the water and sugar in a saucepan. Dissolve the sugar over a low heat, then bring to the boil and cook briskly for about 5 minutes.

Meanwhile, thinly peel and core the apples. Drop them into a bowl of cold salted water to prevent discoloration until all are ready. Rinse the apples and add to the hot syrup. Cook fairly fast for 8 minutes, turning once after 4 minutes, so that the apples cook evenly and become rather transparent in appearance.

Add the lemon juice and pared lemon rind. Simmer for a further 3 minutes, then remove from the heat and leave until quite cold. Serve the apples in their syrup.

FRENCH APPLE PUDDING
APPLES WITH ALMONDS AND CREAM

The original recipe observes, 'this dish differs very little from the English apple pie, when custard has been put to it. Custard and apple pie is the Shibboleth by which an Alderman may be known'; however, you don't have to be an alderman to enjoy this good pudding. It has interesting links with some medieval recipes through the combination of apples and almonds, but it is not at all like apple pie.

Serves 4

2 lb (¾ kg) dessert apples
sugar to taste
3-4 tablespoons (45-60 ml) water
4 oz (115 g) blanched almonds

3-4 bitter almonds (optional)
¼ pint (142 ml) cream
1 egg
2 teaspoons (10 ml) caster sugar

Peel, core and slice the apples. Put them in a saucepan with the sugar to taste and sufficient water to prevent them from sticking. Cover and simmer gently for about 10-15 minutes, or until the apple slices are quite tender.

Put the blanched sweet and the bitter almonds through an electric grinder. Turn into a bowl and stir in the cream. Separate the egg and stir the yolk into the almond mixture. Lightly whisk the egg white and fold into the mixture along with the sugar.

Spoon the cooked apples into an ovenproof dish. Pour the almond mixture over the apples and spread evenly. Set in a slow oven (150°C, 300°F, Gas 2) and bake for 30 minutes.

Serve hot with cream.

VICTORIA PLUM, APRICOT, PEACH OR NECTARINE PUDDING
A DELICATE BAKED PUDDING OF FRUIT WITH EGGS AND CREAM

This is a delectable sweet. The nineteenth-century cook says it may also be 'an iced pudding', but we think the use of breadcrumbs means that it is best eaten while still warm. Many dishes of this time were served in 'a paste border' or with borders of fried bread or toast cut into tiny triangles and fixed with egg white round the edges of the serving dish. This is one that recommends a paste border; a strip of pastry, the same depth as the filling, may be laid round as a wall before the pudding mixture is poured in.

Serves 4

2 oz (55 g) fresh white breadcrumbs
½ pint (284 ml) double cream
2 egg yolks
1 tablespoon (15 ml) white wine
1 heaped tablespoon (17.25 ml) caster sugar

12 whole Victoria plums or 8 large apricots or 4 whole peaches or nectarines
1 egg white

Put the breadcrumbs in a bowl. Heat the cream in a saucepan until almost boiling. Pour over the crumbs and stir to blend. Cover the bowl and leave until cool. Then stir in the egg yolks, wine and sugar.

Poach the fruit in a little water until barely tender, then drain. When cool enough to handle, skin the fruit and remove the stones. Press the flesh through a coarse sieve or food mill to make a purée. Stir the purée into the cream and breadcrumb mixture. Whisk the egg white until stiff and fold into the mixture. Pour into a lightly greased, shallow, ovenproof dish. Set in a moderate oven (180°C, 350°F, Gas 4) and bake for 40 minutes. Serve hot with a bowl of lightly whipped cream.

CONTINENTAL RECIPES FROM THE SEVENTEENTH CENTURY

The seventeenth century brought about great changes in the style of cooking and choice of ingredients. The new fashion in food started in Italy and spread north and west to other countries in Europe, reaching its highest peak in France in the nineteenth and the present century with their internationally famous *haute cuisine*. Seventeenth century cooks abandoned the lavish medieval use of spices and flavoured their dishes more subtly. Sauces were more delicate, butter was used instead of lard or oil, and they were thickened and enriched with eggs. Sugar became cheaper and more available and replaced honey as a sweetener.

RAMEQUIN AU FROMAGE
SAVOURY CHEESE TOASTS WITH ONION

At the beginning of *The French Cook* 'Englished' by IDG in 1653, there is a glossary of those untranslateable French culinary terms with which IDG thought his readers would be unfamiliar. He translates *ramequin* as 'a kind of toste' as it is in this recipe. An early French dictionary gives *ramequin* as ramekin-dish of cheese, etc; so, perhaps, ramekin is a comparatively recent term for the pottery dish. The final instructions in the old recipe are to 'pass a fire-shovel over it red hot', a minute or two under a very hot grill works in much the same way.

Serves 4

2 oz (55 g) butter	salt
1 medium onion, finely chopped	freshly milled black pepper
4 oz (115 g) grated Cheddar cheese	4 slices bread

Heat the butter in a saucepan and fry the onion until turning yellow. Add the grated cheese, a little salt and plenty of black pepper (the original advises 'pepper in abundance'). Beat the mixture with a wooden spoon over a fairly high heat until the cheese has melted and is smooth. Have ready four slices of bread toasted on one side, spread the cheese mixture onto the bread side of each slice and put under a hot grill until brown.

96

EIN KAPPAUNEN WEISZ
A PIQUANT WHITE SAUCE FOR POULTRY

The sauce for the chicken in this German recipe which dates from the beginning of the seventeenth century is of such excellence that it is hard to believe how long ago it was invented. It has a certain similarity to Sauce Béarnaise in the ingredients and flavour, and it is a lot quicker and easier to make. Its piquant delicacy lifts a roast chicken into the realms of *haute cuisine*.

Serves 4-6

1 chicken, about 3½ lb (1½ kg)
1 oz (30 g) butter
½ pint (284 ml) chicken stock

For the sauce
2 egg yolks
½ pint (284 ml) beef stock
2 oz (55 g) butter
1 tablespoon (15 ml) chopped fresh parsley
1 teaspoon (5 ml) chopped fresh thyme, or ½ teaspoon (2.5 ml) dried
1 teaspoon (5 ml) chopped fresh tarragon, or ½ teaspoon (2.5 ml) dried
1 tablespoon (15 ml) wine vinegar
salt and pepper

French roast the chicken by rubbing the butter over the bird, covering the breast with foil and setting it in a roasting tin with the chicken stock. Place in a hot oven (200°C, 400°F, Gas 6) and roast it for 1¼ hours.

About 10 minutes before the end of the roasting time prepare the sauce. Lightly beat the egg yolks in a small bowl and stir in the beef stock. Pour into a small pan and set over low heat. Add the butter in small pieces and stir constantly while the mixture thickens. Remove from the heat, stir in the chopped herbs and the vinegar slowly. Return to a low heat, season with salt and pepper and stir briskly until the sauce is nearly boiling (do not boil). Remove from the heat. Carve the chicken and arrange the pieces on a hot serving dish. Pour over the sauce and serve.

ANATRE AROSTA
DUCK STUFFED WITH FRUIT, SERVED WITH TAGLIATELLI

The original Italian recipe was cooked with wild duck, and when in season these should be used, with a combination of fruits also in season. Alternative combinations of fruit can be used with domestic duck: the original stuffing was given as 'various fruits' with sliced lemons. Dried apricots and lemons are good in winter, green gooseberries with orange for spring, cherries and redcurrants for summer, well-spiced apples with walnuts for autumn. The duck would have needed to be properly carved and was probably beautifully arranged on a dish. At this time carving was an art which had to be learned and in all the princely houses it was the preserve of the gentry.

Serves 4

1 duck, about 3-4 lb (1½-1¾ kg)
4 oz (115 g) dried apricots, soaked
overnight
thinly pared rind of ½ lemon
1 peeled lemon

For serving
¾ lb (340 g) tagliatelli
lemon wedges

Prick the breast of the duck with a fork. Drain the soaked apricots and reserve the liquid. Stuff the duck with the apricots, the lemon rind and the sliced lemon flesh from which all pith and pips have been removed.

Put the duck in a roasting tin and add 4 tablespoons (60 ml) of the liquid in which the apricots were soaked. Roast in a moderately hot oven (190°C, 375°F, Gas 5), allowing 30 minutes per 1 lb (455 g). When ready, the skin should be well crisped and brown. Meanwhile, cook the tagliatelli in a saucepan of boiling salted water for 10-12 minutes or until tender; then drain well and keep hot.

Lift the duck on to a serving dish. Pour a few spoonfuls of the pan juices over the tagliatelli and turn well to mix both together. Serve the tagliatelli beside the duck with the apricot stuffing spooned out and arranged on the tagliatelli. Add a garnish of lemon wedges.

REINS DE MOUTON
TENDER CHOPS WITH A PIQUANT CAPER SAUCE

In this seventeenth century French recipe, as with many old recipes using mutton in the title, mutton really does mean mutton and not the young, tender lamb that we know. Nowadays, it is almost impossible to buy meat from an older animal which, for all its tendency to toughness, has an especially good flavour and requires special treatment. This dish requires the meat to be simmered after first browning it in fat, and by reducing the cooking time for the tender chops from a loin of lamb you can achieve much the same result.

Serves 6-8

1 loin of lamb, 8 or 10 bones
seasoned flour (see below)
butter or lard (see below)
1½ pints (850 ml) stock
bouquet garni
1 teaspoon (5 ml) salt
½ teaspoon (2.5 ml) freshly milled black pepper
¼ teaspoon (1.25 ml) ground cloves
¼ teaspoon (1.25 ml) ground mace

For the sauce
1 medium onion
1 oz (30 g) butter
1 tablespoon (15 ml) flour
½ tablespoon (7.25 ml) wine vinegar (white or red)
2 tablespoons (30 ml) capers

Cut the loin into separate chops and, if very fatty, trim off surplus fat. Dust each chop with seasoned flour, heat some butter or lard in a large saucepan and fry the chops on both sides until brown. Add the stock, the bouquet garni and seasonings, cover the pan and cook gently for 1 hour (longer if the meat is tough). Meanwhile finely chop the onion, heat the butter in a small pan and fry the onion until turning brown. Stir in the flour to make a roux, then add some hot stock from the pan of chops to make a thick sauce and add the vinegar and capers. Dish up the chops and stir the remaining gravy into the pan of sauce. Pour the sauce over the chops and serve hot.

ROGNONE DI VITELLA IN CROSTATE
KIDNEY PIE WITH HAM AND CURD CHEESE

Fresh buffalo milk cheese was used in the original recipe for this substantial kidney pie. We have substituted cream or curd cheese. Thinly sliced dry cured ham, such as Parma ham, may also have been used and, if you wish to be extravagant, it would no doubt enhance the flavour. This pie would have been eaten with a knife and fork, as forks came into ordinary use in Italy and Spain in the sixteenth century though not until a hundred years later in Germany, France and England. In Byzantine high society they must have been used much earlier for the Venetians were scandalised when the son of a doge of Venice married a lady from Constantinople who ate her food with two-pronged golden forks instead of her fingers.

Serves 4-6

12 lambs' kidneys	*salt and freshly milled black pepper*
6 tablespoons (90 ml) stock	*4 thin slices cooked ham*
3-4 oz (85-115 g) cream or curd cheese	*8 oz (225 g) shortcrust pastry (page 75)*
2 teaspoons (10 ml) lemon juice	*made with 8 oz (225 g) flour and 4 oz*
	(115 g) fat

Snip the core from each kidney, but leave the kidneys whole. Remove the skin and put the kidneys in a saucepan with the stock. Bring to the boil, cover and simmer for about 10 minutes until they are just cooked. Remove from the pan and reserve the stock. Dice the kidneys and place in a clean saucepan, adding 2 tablespoons (30 ml) of the reserved stock. Add the cream cheese and stir over a low heat until the cheese has melted. Add the lemon juice, season with salt and pepper and draw off the heat. Finely chop the ham.

Divide the pastry in two. Roll out one piece and use to line an 8-9 in (20-22.5 cm) pie plate. Damp the pastry rim. Sprinkle the chopped ham over the base and pour the kidney mixture in to fill the pie. Roll out the remaining pastry and cover the pie. Trim and press edges well to seal. Make a hole in the centre of the lid. Place in a moderately hot oven (190°C, 375°F, Gas 5) and bake for 30-40 minutes, or until nicely browned. Serve hot.

LINGUA DI VITELLI
LAMBS' TONGUES WITH MIXED VEGETABLES AND FRUITS

The combination of the flavour of Seville orange and various fruits and vegetables in this early Italian dish of tongue is very unusal. If Seville oranges are unobtainable, a mixture of sweet orange and lemon juice is very good. The original used calves' tongues, but nowadays an ox tongue and lambs' tongues are usually sold. This dish requires long, slow cooking but the result is melting, tender and fragrant.

Serves 4

8 lambs' tongues
bouquet garni
4-6 black peppercorns
2 oz (55 g) dried figs, soaked overnight
2 oz (55 g) dried apricots, soaked
overnight
3 rashers streaky bacon
6 tablespoons (90 ml) stock
6 tablespoons (90 ml) dry white wine

3 cloves
½ level teaspoon (2.5 ml) ground
cinnamon
salt and freshly milled black pepper
juice of 1 Seville orange or juice of ½
sweet orange and ½ lemon
2-3 pieces thinly pared orange rind
8 artichoke hearts, fresh or canned
¼ pint (142 ml) shelled peas

Put the tongues in a large saucepan with plenty of fresh cold water to cover. Add the bouquet garni and peppercorns and bring to the boil. Skim, then cover and cook gently for 1½ hours, or until tender. Test by piercing the tongue with a sharp knife at the tip. Lift the tongues from the pan and plunge into cold water. Peel away the skin and remove the bone and gristle at the root of each one.

Drain the soaked figs and apricots and place in the bottom of a smaller pan or fireproof casserole. Add the trimmed bacon rashers cut in half, the stock, wine, cloves, cinnamon, salt and pepper, the strained orange juice and a few shreds or orange rind. Place the tongues on top. Cover the pan tightly and bring slowly to the boil. Simmer for 10 minutes then transfer the pan to a slow oven (150°C, 300°F, Gas 2) and cook for one hour. Add the artichoke hearts and peas and cook for a further 20-30 minutes.

Serve the tongues on the bed of vegetables and fruits with juices from the pan poured over.

OMELET PERSIL Á L'OIGNON
AN OMELETTE WITH PARSLEY AND SWEET ONION

Frayzes or omelettes were popular in both France and England from the Middle Ages; usually they were savoury, as sweet ones were called tansies or pan perdies (from pain perdu) and a froise seems to have been a fritter. Ever since people started cooking omelettes they have held strongly individual ideas as to the best method, and debates about beating times, adding water or milk and length of cooking have continued for centuries. The seemingly strange instructions in this old recipe to sprinkle a savoury omelette with sugar should be followed as it enhances the sweet onion flavour and balances the richness of the eggs in a way that is really very good.

Serves 4

6 large eggs
1 small onion, or 2 shallots, finely chopped
1 tablespoon (15 ml) chopped parsley
1 oz (30 g) melted butter

salt and freshly milled black pepper
a little butter for frying
caster sugar

Break the eggs into a bowl and mix lightly with a fork. Add the onion to the eggs along with the chopped parsley, melted butter and salt and pepper. Heat a small knob of butter in a large omelette pan and, when very hot, pour in the egg mixture, stir and cook the omelette in the usual way, roll up and cut into 4 rounds. Sprinkle lightly with a little caster sugar and serve immediately.

TOPINAMBOURS
FRIED ARTICHOKE SLICES WITH ONION

The story of how these vegetables acquired their name is an interesting one. In the 17th century Jerusalem artichokes were introduced into Europe from North America where they grow wild. In Italy they were called *girasole*, sunflower artichokes, to distinguish them from the globe variety. *Girasole* became corrupted into Jerusalem in English. The French call them *topinambours*. In 1613 the French court had its first sight of some members of the Brazilian tribe of Tupinamba, which created great interest, and they called the new vegetable *topinambours* in the hope that it would be as great a success as the Tupinamba. In such a way are names created.

The old recipe advised roasting the artichokes before skinning them, but this is an extremely difficult process. In Perigord they still eat *les topinambours en beignets* and advise cooking the vegetable in boiling salted water before peeling them and slicing them, then dipping the slices in batter before frying them in deep fat.

Serves 4

1 lb (455 g) Jerusalem artichokes
½ oz (15 g) butter
1 medium onion, finely chopped

salt and freshly milled black pepper
1 teaspoon (5 ml) wine vinegar
grating of nutmeg

Wash the artichokes and trim off the whiskers. Put them in a pan of boiling salted water and cook for ten minutes. Peel off the skins as soon as they are cool enough to handle and allow to cool.

Melt the butter in a large frying pan, fry the onion gently until soft, but not brown; add salt and plenty of pepper. Cut the artichokes into thick slices and fry them with the onion until golden – like sauté potatoes. Sprinkle with vinegar and nutmeg and serve hot from the pan.

NIMB LINSE
ONION-FLAVOURED LENTILS WITH BACON AND HERBS

The German title of this 17th century recipe literally means 'Take lentils'. When you cook them according to the instructions they are very good indeed. With chopped bacon and plenty of herbs they make a delicious supper dish for a cold night, or a weekend lunch at home with beer, and bread and cheese. They keep hot or reheat easily. Use brown or green lentils for this recipe, for they are so much nicer than the slightly bitter yellow ones.

Serves 4

8 oz (225 g) dried lentils
1 pint (568 ml) beef stock
1 large onion, peeled and chopped
2 cloves garlic, crushed
½ level teaspoon (2.5 ml) salt
freshly milled black pepper
4 oz (115 g) boiled bacon or ham
2 tablespoons (30 ml) chopped fresh parsley

1 teaspoon (5 ml) chopped fresh marjoram, or ½ teaspoon (2.5 ml) dried
1 teaspoon (5 ml) chopped fresh tarragon, or ½ teaspoon (2.5 ml) dried
1 teaspoon (5 ml) chopped fresh chervil, or ½ teaspoon (2.5 ml) dried

Wash the lentils and put in a large saucepan. Add the beef stock and bring to the boil. Add the onions and garlic to the lentils with the salt and a seasoning of pepper. Cover and cook gently for about 1 hour, or until the lentils are quite soft. Drain and reserve about 3 tablespoons (45 ml) of the liquid from the pan.

Cut the bacon into small dice and put in a clean saucepan with the cooked lentils, chopped herbs and the reserved liquid. Stir and cook for a few minutes to thoroughly heat through. Serve hot.

SPENAT TURTEN
SPINACH TART WITH CHEESE AND BREADCRUMBS

Parmesan cheese and mace give a special flavour to this spinach tart which is enriched with egg yolks and butter. It is taken from Max Rumpolt's book *Ein neu Kochbuch* which is accepted as the first outside Renaissance Italy to include the more refined way of cooking from which the classic French cuisine developed.

Serves 4

1 lb (455 g) spinach
2 oz (55 g) fresh white breadcrumbs
1 tablespoon (15 ml) grated Parmesan cheese
½ level teaspoon (2.5 ml) ground mace
¼ level teaspoon (1.25 ml) freshly milled black pepper

pinch of salt
2 egg yolks
2 oz (55 g) butter
6 oz (170 g) shortcrust pastry (page 75)

Remove the stems and wash the spinach in plenty of cold water. Drain and cook, with no additional water, for about 10 minutes, or until just tender. Drain well and chop roughly. Put the chopped spinach in a bowl with the breadcrumbs, Parmesan cheese, mace, pepper and salt. Mix well together. Lightly beat the egg yolks and stir into the spinach mixture. Melt the butter in a small pan and pour half of it into the spinach. Stir to mix the ingredients.

Roll out the pastry on a floured surface and use to line an 8-in (20-cm) pie plate. Fill with the spinach mixture and pour over the rest of the melted butter. Set in a moderate oven (190°C, 350°F, Gas 4) and bake for 30-40 minutes until the pastry is cooked. Serve hot.

TARTE AUX PRUNIERS DE DAMAS
DAMSON TART WITH A CREAMY TOPPING

Damsons have a decided tang which is mellowed by the delicious pinkish-purple filling of sweet juice and whipped cream which covers them. The tart base in the original recipe was to be made of either 'fine paste' or puff paste, the instructions for making the latter were identical to those in any modern cookery book, including distributing the pieces of butter over a third of the paste, folding, rolling and repeating three times. M. de La Varenne whose recipe this was, left the reader with no illusions about an easy method, but warned him not to deceive himself as to the difficulties of making puff pastry.

Serves 4-6

1 lb (450 g) damsons
4 tablespoons (60 ml) sugar
½ pint (284 ml) red wine
½ teaspoon (2.5 ml) ground ginger
½ teaspoon (2.5 ml) ground cinnamon
¼ pint (142 ml) double cream

For the puff pastry
8 oz (225 g) strong white flour
¼ teaspoon (1.25 ml) cream of tartar
pinch of salt
1 oz (25 g) white cooking fat
6-8 tablespoons (90-112 ml) cold water
7 oz (200 g) butter

Sift the flour, cream of tartar and salt into a mixing bowl. Add the cooking fat in pieces and rub in with the fingertips. Add the water and mix to a rough dough with a fork. Turn on to a floured work surface and knead dough lightly once or twice to remove the cracks. Wrap in cling film and chill for 30 minutes.

Sprinkle the butter with flour and roll out or shape into a neat rectangle about ½ in (1 cm) thick. Roll out the chilled dough to a rectangle about ½ in (1 cm) wider than the butter and slightly more than three times as long. Place butter in centre and fold the pastry over to enclose it completely. Gently press the open edges with the rolling pin to seal. (This is the first roll and fold.)

Give the dough a half turn to bring sealed ends to the top and bottom. Press dough gently with rolling pin, moving it from centre to top, then from centre to bottom to distribute the air. With quick light strokes roll out the dough to a rectangle three times as long as it is wide. Fold the bottom third up over the centre and the top third down. Seal edges again. Wrap and chill the pastry

for 30 minutes. Repeat the rolling, folding and sealing twice, then chill for 30 minutes and repeat rolling, folding and sealing twice again to make a total of six times. Chill for 10 minutes before finally rolling out to line an 8-in (20-cm) flan ring. Prick the base and cover with greaseproof paper, half-fill with rice or dried beans and bake 'blind' in a hot oven (220°C, 425°F, Gas 7) for 20 minutes. Remove paper and beans and return to the oven for a further 10 minutes, or until the pastry has lightly browned and has dried out.

Wash the damsons and remove any stalks. Make a syrup by gently heating the sugar and wine together, stir until the sugar has dissolved, then boil for 5 minutes. Remove from the heat and stir in the ginger and cinnamon.

Poach the damsons in this syrup for a few minutes until just tender, but still whole. Drain the damsons from the syrup and arrange them over the pastry case. Boil up the syrup until it has reduced and thickened and leave to cool. Whip the cream, then whisk in the cooled syrup, spoon over the damsons and serve.

PASTICETTI DI DIVERSE CONSERVE DI FRUTTI
A MIXED FRUIT PIE FOR ALL SEASONS

The filling for the pie in the original version of this Italian recipe was made with green gooseberries and red apples with a conserve of mixed fruits such as raisins, almonds and walnuts with spices as an alternative filling. Candied or crystallized fruits soaked overnight in a little wine to plump and soften them are nice as a filling, with some of the reserved wine liquid added.

Serves 4

8 oz (225 g) plain flour
2 oz (55 g) lard, cut in pieces
2 oz (55 g) butter, cut in pieces
2 oz (55 g) sifted icing sugar
2 egg yolks
2 tablespoons (30 ml) water
For the glaze
1 egg white and caster sugar to dredge

For the filling
6 red dessert apples
½ teaspoon (2.5 ml) cinnamon
1 lb (455 g) green gooseberries, topped and tailed
2 tablespoons (30 ml) caster sugar

Sift the flour into a mixing bowl. Add the lard and butter and rub into the flour. Add the icing sugar, mix and make a well in the centre. Break the egg yolks into it, mix with a fork, adding enough water to make a firm dough. Roll into a ball and set aside for an hour in a cold place.

Divide the pastry into two pieces, one a little larger, for the top. Roll out the smaller piece to line a greased 8-in (20-cm) pie plate. Core and slice the apples, leaving the skins on. Spread a layer of apples and gooseberries on the pastry base, sprinkle with cinnamon and sugar, then add another layer of fruit. Roll out the remaining pastry for the pie top, damp the edges and seal. Cut 2 or 3 slits in the top. Bake in the middle of a moderately hot oven (190°C, 375°F, Gas 4) for 40 minutes or until the pastry is cooked.

Meanwhile, make the glaze by lightly beating the egg white. When the pastry is cooked, remove from the oven, brush on the egg white and dredge with caster sugar. Return to the oven for a few minutes to brown the top.

NIMB GERIEBENE MADELN
PASTRIES FILLED WITH RAISINS AND ALMOND PASTE

These little German pastries have a sweet filling of almonds and raisins gently scented with rosewater. Though less highly spiced, they are similar to some medieval puddings, dating from about 300 years earlier, which were made with dried fruits such as figs, dates and raisins.

Serves 4

2 oz (55 g) ground almonds
4 oz (115 g) raisins or currants
2 oz (55 g) caster sugar
2 teaspoons (10 ml) rosewater

6 oz (170 g) shortcrust pastry
(page 75)
1 oz (30 g) butter

Mix the ground almonds, raisins and sugar in a bowl and stir in the rosewater. Using the hands, mould the mixture into a long 'rope' and cut into 16 small pieces. Shape each one into a little roll.

Roll out the pastry on a floured surface and cut into rounds the size of a small saucer, or into rectangles. Put a portion of the almond mixture on each piece of pastry. Damp edges and fold over to enclose the filling. Seal the edges neatly.

Melt the butter in a shallow baking tray so that it is well greased and place the pastries on the baking tin. Set in a moderate oven (190°C, 350°F, Gas 4) and bake for 20 minutes. Sprinkle with caster sugar and serve hot.

Tarte aux Amandes
FRUIT TART WITH ALMOND BASE AND CUSTARD TOPPING

Massepin, or massepain, was marzipan, and the old recipe gave only a mixture of ground almonds and sugar to make the paste; this does not bind together although in the old days they would have used whole almonds pounded to a paste, which would have been more oily. So strongly does this recipe suggest that it was a forerunner of present-day French *tartes* or *tartelettes* (which are made with *paté sucrée*, a rich short mixture and filled with *crème patissière*, confectioner's custard, then topped with fruit) that we took the liberty of adding some butter to the almond mixture in order to bind it together. The original gave raspberries, strawberries or cherries which should be used raw for the filling, with gooseberries or dried apricots as an alternative (these should be lightly stewed to keep their shape) and the apricots first soaked for several hours.

Serves 4-6

½ lb (225 g) ground almonds
¼ lb (115 g) caster sugar
1½ oz (45 g) softened butter
½ pint (284 ml) milk
½ tablespoon (2.5 ml) plain flour
½ oz (15 g) butter

1 whole egg, 1 egg separated
pinch of salt
3 tablespoons (7.5 ml) sugar
½ lb (225 g) fresh or frozen raspberries
(or gooseberries or dried apricots)

Put the ground almonds and sugar into a basin, mix together with a wooden spoon, then work in the softened butter with your fingertips as if making a crumble. Knead into a ball and line an oiled 9-in (22.5-cm) pie plate with the paste to a depth of at least ½ in (1 cm). Pressing it well down and against the sides, but not onto the rim or it will scorch. Bake in a low oven (100°C, 200°F, Gas ¼) for 40 minutes, after which the paste will still be soft.

Prepare a custard by adding a little of the milk to the flour in a saucepan. (The old recipe described this as making 'a cream with milk'.) Mix to a smooth cream, then put the pan over a low heat and add the rest of the milk gradually, stirring continuously until the mixture comes to the boil. Remove from the heat and stir in the ½ oz (15 g) of butter. Break the whole egg into a basin and add the other yolk, then lightly whisk together with the salt and a tablespoon (15 ml) of the sugar. When the milk mixture has cooled a little, pour it onto the eggs, whisking all the time, then strain back into the pan and stir over low heat until the custard thickens (do not boil). Remove from the heat and pour the custard into the almond paste case. Cover the tart with foil and return to the oven (150°C, 300°F, Gas 2) for about 35 minutes, until the custard has set and the paste is firm and golden.

Arrange the fruit over the baked custard, whisk the egg white stiffly, fold in the remaining 2 tablespoons (30 ml) of sugar and spoon this mixture over the fruit. Bake in a hot oven (200°C, 400°F, Gas 6) for 5 minutes until the meringue has coloured and set.

AUSTRALIAN RECIPES FROM THE EIGHTEENTH AND NINETEENTH CENTURIES

MURRAY TURNOVERS
PASTRIES FILLED WITH FISH, VEGETABLES AND EGGS

An early Australian picnic tended to be a community affair, with everyone in the neighbourhood attending and everyone contributing something to the feast. These plump triangles of crisp pastry stuffed with a moist filling of fish, eggs and vegetables were a meal in themselves. They make a great addition to a modern picnic, or a main dish for the family, when served with a nicely-dressed green salad.

Serves 6

½ lb (225 g) shortcrust pastry (page 75)
7 oz (200 g) canned tuna, drained, or any firm cooked fish
2 tomatoes, finely chopped
1 small onion, finely chopped
2 hard-boiled eggs, chopped
2 tablespoons (30 ml) snipped chives or shredded green part of a leek
4 tablespoons (60 ml) fresh white breadcrumbs
light sprinkling sea salt
plenty of freshly milled black pepper

Roll out the pastry to a large square no more than ¼ in (½ cm) thick; allow to rest while preparing the filling.

Flake the fish into a bowl, and add the remaining ingredients. Either pile the mixture onto one side of the pastry square, or cut the pastry into six smaller squares each about 5 in (13 cm) square and fill each with some of the fish mixture. Seal the edges with a little cold water. Make a few slits in the top of the turnover and brush the surface with milk. Bake in a hot oven (230°C, 450°F, Gas 8) for 20-25 minutes, until the pastry is cooked. Serve warm, or cold.

DARLING RIVER STEAK
BAKED STEAKS STUFFED WITH APPLES

In the cattle-rearing regions of Victoria and New South Wales, the farmers had plenty of prime beef for their family meals. In this recipe, the apple stuffing gives an unusual sharpness and freshness to the juicy, satisfying steaks.

Serves 4

1½ lbs (¾ kg) rump steak	2 teaspoons (10 ml) brown sugar
1 large cooking apple	salt and freshly milled black pepper
2 oz (55 g) butter	1 oz (30 g) fresh white breadcrumbs

Trim steak and cut into two pieces. Cut each piece through horizontally to make a pocket. Peel, core and coarsely chop the apple into a bowl. Melt the butter and pour half over the apple, add the brown sugar and seasoning. Fill the steaks with this mixture. Brush over an ovenproof dish with some of the butter and add the steaks. Cover with breadcrumbs and trickle over the remaining butter. Cover the dish with greaseproof paper and cook in a moderate oven (180°C, 350°F, Gas 4) for 1 hour, removing the paper for the last 10 minutes. Slice the two pieces of steak across to make four, and serve from the dish with gravy.

MISTER MUSGROVE'S LAMB
RICHLY STUFFED LAMB BAKED IN FLAKY PASTRY

We don't know who Mr Musgrove was, but Mrs Musgrove must have been a spectacularly good cook. Maybe he was a well-to-do batchelor, a sheep farmer with a taste for gourmet cooking. Whatever the background history of the dish, it is an all-time winner: a boned leg of lamb stuffed with kidneys, mushrooms and herbs with brandy, the whole then wrapped in a fragile jacket of flaky pastry and baked *en croûte* to a crisp perfection.

Serves 6

1 small leg of lamb, about 3½ lb (1½ kg) boned
4 lambs' kidneys
4 oz (115 g) mushrooms
butter (see below)
1½ teaspoon (7.5 ml) chopped fresh thyme, or 1 teaspoon (5 ml) dried
1 teaspoon (5 ml) chopped fresh rosemary, or ½ teaspoon dried

salt and freshly milled black pepper
2 tablespoons (30 ml) fresh breadcrumbs
2 tablespoons (30 ml) brandy
1¼ lb (½ kg) flaky pastry (page 117)
1 egg

Skin the kidneys and snip out the cores, lightly fry in a little butter for a minute or two. Add the peeled, sliced mushrooms and fry gently for another 2 minutes, then add the thyme, rosemary, salt, pepper and breadcrumbs. Remove from the heat and stir in the brandy. When cool enough to handle, dice the kidneys and stuff the lamb with the mixture. Roll up the joint and tie securely with string. Roast in a hot oven 220°C, 425°F, Gas 7 for 1 hour. Pour off any excess fat from the roasting tin.

Allow to cool then brush over with some melted butter, seasoned with salt and pepper. Roll out the pastry thinly and wrap round the joint, sealing the joins with a little cold water. Brush the pastry all over with water and continue to bake in the hot oven in the same pan. After 30 minutes brush over the pastry with a little lightly beaten egg and return to the oven for a further 15 minutes, until the pastry is golden brown.

GOLDEN CHICKEN SALAD
A CHICKEN MAYONNAISE SALAD WITH FRUITS

Perhaps this Australian dish was an early version of the well-known *Coronation Chicken*. It has the same creamy, curry-flavoured mayonnaise as a sauce for cold chicken, but the mingled tropical fruits and crisp vegetables make it a much more interesting recipe. Whatever its origins, it is an ideal dish for scorching summer heat. A hint of spicy curry to whet the appetite and plenty of refreshing raw ingredients which, when the temperature soars, don't require the cook to spend too long in the kitchen.

Serves 4

12 oz (340 g) diced, cooked chicken meat
20 fresh lychees, peeled and stoned; or tinned lychees drained and stoned
segments of 2 mandarins, or tinned mandarins, drained
½ cucumber, peeled and diced
3 tomatoes, peeled and chopped
3 sticks celery, washed and finely sliced
1 small onion, or 3 shallots, finely chopped

1 fat clove garlic, peeled and crushed
salt and freshly milled black pepper
2 teaspoons (10 ml) curry powder
2 tablespoons (30 ml) vegetable oil
½ tablespoon (7.5 ml) wine vinegar
mayonnaise (see below)

Put the chicken meat into a large bowl. Cut the lychees into small pieces. Peel the mandarins and separate the segments. Put the chicken and fruit into a large bowl and add the cucumber, tomatoes, celery, onion, garlic, seasoning and curry powder. Mix together with a fork, then add the oil and vinegar and mix again. Finally add enough mayonnaise to lightly coat all the ingredients, stir gently and turn into a clean glass bowl. Serve cold, but not chilled.

RABBIT PIE
RABBIT PIE COOKED WITH BEER, HERBS AND STUFFED PRUNES

The Australians turned their national pest to good advantage in this country recipe, using home-brewed beer for the cooking liquid to make a wonderfully rich gravy. Stuffed prunes are a delicious addition and although the original recipe included hard-boiled eggs, we found they add nothing to the pie in flavour or texture, so unless you want to follow the old recipe closely, you could omit the eggs without harm.

Serves 4

1 rabbit
1 tablespoon (15 ml) vinegar
1 bay leaf
1 blade mace
2 sprigs parsley
2 sprigs thyme
2 medium onions
8 rashers streaky bacon
a little dripping
about ½ pint (284 ml) beer
salt and freshly milled black pepper
12 large prunes, cooked
½ lb (225 g) flaky pastry (see below)

Stuffing for prunes
2 oz (55 g) breadcrumbs
2 tablespoons (30 ml) finely chopped onion
1 oz (30 g) finely chopped walnuts
2 tablespoons (30 ml) finely chopped parsley
4 hardboiled eggs (optional)

Put the rabbit in a deep dish and cover it with cold, salted water. Add the vinegar, bay leaf, mace, parsley and thyme. Soak the rabbit for several hours or overnight. Turn the rabbit once half way through soaking time. Drain the rabbit, pat dry with a paper towel and cut into neat joints. Peel and finely slice the onions, remove bacon rind and cut the rashers into small squares. Heat dripping in a saucepan and fry the onion slices and bacon until starting to brown. Add the rabbit pieces and brown on both sides. Pour over enough beer to nearly cover the rabbit, season with salt and pepper, cover the pan and simmer gently for 1½ hours, until the rabbit is tender.

Meanwhile, make the pastry and then prepare the stuffed prunes. Put all the ingredients for the stuffing into a small bowl and mix with a little prune juice to bind. Make a small slit in each prune and carefully remove the stone. Fill the prunes with small teaspoonfuls of the mixture and reshape them.

When the rabbit is tender, lift from the pan and remove as many bones as you can. Pack the pieces into a deep pie dish, with the stuffed prunes and sliced hard boiled eggs arranged between them. Season with salt and pepper and pour over the gravy from the pan to come halfway up the pie dish. Cover with a pastry lid, make a hole in the centre and brush over with milk. Decorate with pastry leaves cut from the trimmings. Bake in the centre of a hot oven (200°C, 400°F, Gas 6) for 30 minutes, until the pastry is well risen and golden brown.

FLAKY PASTRY

8 oz (225 g) plain flour
pinch of salt
6 oz (175 g) butter

6-8 tablespoons (90-112 ml) cold water
squeeze of lemon juice

Sift the flour and salt into a mixing bowl. Cut butter in ½ in (1 cm) cubes and add to the flour. Alternatively, have fat thoroughly chilled and grate on a coarse grater directly on to flour. Dip fat in the flour as you grate to keep the pieces separate. Mix flour and pieces of fat with the fingertips to separate lumps of fat but do *not* rub it into the flour.

Add the water and lemon juice and lightly mix to a soft dough with a table knife, keeping pieces of fat whole. Turn on to a floured surface (do not knead) and roll out to a rectangle three times as long as it is wide. Fold the bottom third of the pastry over the centre, then fold the top third down. Gently press the open ends to seal and give the dough a half turn to bring sealed ends to the top and bottom. Repeat the rolling, folding and sealing. Wrap in cling film and chill for 30 minutes. Repeat rolling, folding and sealing twice more to make a total of four times.

CAULIFLOWER BAKE
CAULIFLOWER AND HAM LAYERED IN A SOUR CREAM AND CHEESE SAUCE

More tasty and substantial than cauliflower *au gratin*, this satisfying dish was served for high tea, or supper, or whenever the day's work was done. For busy people today, it makes a flavourful light lunch with a cool glass of Australian wine.

Serves 4

1 medium cauliflower
4 oz (115 g) diced cooked ham
2 oz (55 g) butter
1 medium onion
2 egg yolks
1 tablespoon (15 ml) chopped parsley
¼ teaspoon (1.25 ml) grated nutmeg

freshly milled black pepper
small pot (5 oz) sour cream
2 tablespoons (30 ml) milk
5 tablespoons (75 ml) grated cheddar cheese
paprika

Trim away the outside leaves of the cauliflower and break into flowerets, slice some of the stalk finely and keep the small tender leaves. Cook cauliflower in lightly salted boiling water for 5 minutes. Drain. Grease a shallow ovenproof dish with half the butter. Scatter a layer of ham over the bottom of the dish, add a layer of cauliflower, another layer of ham, and finish with a layer of cauliflower. Dot with the remaining butter. Chop the onion finely and mix in a basin with the egg yolks, parsley, nutmeg and black pepper, stir in the soured cream and milk and mix thoroughly, then pour over the cauliflower. Top with grated cheese and a sprinkling of paprika. Bake in a moderate over (180°C, 350°F, Gas 4) for 35 minutes until the cheese topping is brown and bubbly.

BANANA CAKE
AN EASILY MADE CAKE WITH BANANAS AND WALNUTS

A beautifully moist cake that is full of true banana flavour and crunchy walnuts. It is a real family cake just right for eating in large wedges, and although it keeps fresh and moist for a long time, you will find that it disappears fast.

Serves 4-6

3 oz (85 g) butter
6 oz (170 g) sugar
1 egg, beaten
3 bananas
8 oz (225 g) plain flour
1 teaspoon (5 ml) bicarbonate of soda
1 teaspoon (5 ml) baking powder
½ teaspoon (2.5 ml) grated nutmeg
2 tablespoons (30 ml) milk
2 oz (55 g) chopped walnuts

For the glaze
2 oz (55 g) sugar
2 tablespoons (30 ml) water
2 tablespoons (30 ml) lemon juice

Grease and line a 9-in (23-cm) cake tin and set the oven to 180°C, 350°F, Gas 4. Beat butter and sugar together until light and creamy, add the egg gradually and beat well between each addition. Mash the bananas and beat into the mixture a spoonful at a time. Fold in the sifted flour, bicarbonate, baking powder and nutmeg. Stir in the milk and the walnuts and pour the mixture into the cake tin. Bake for 1¼-1½ hours in a moderate oven (180°C, 350°F, Gas 4). After the first ½ hour cover the tin with kitchen foil to prevent the top browning too fast. As soon as the cake looks set, test with a skewer and if cooked, remove it from the oven and turn out, right side up, onto a wire rack.

Make the glaze by dissolving the sugar in the water and lemon juice over a low heat, bring to the boil and simmer for two minutes. While the cake is still warm, brush over the top surface twice with the hot glaze. Leave to cool.

BANANA FRITTERS
BANANAS COOKED IN A LIGHT FLAVOURED BATTER

No penny-pinching recipe this from an early settler's kitchen, but luxury fritters that will earn the cook a compliment.

The bananas are cooked in the lightest of batters flavoured with brandy and dusted with sugar and cinnamon. They are delicious served with whipped cream, or vanilla ice cream.

Serves 4-6

6 or 8 bananas, according to size
oil for frying

For the batter
4 oz (115 g) plain flour
pinch salt
2 eggs
¼ pint (142 ml) milk
1 tablespoon (15 ml) brandy
½ oz (15 g) butter
2 or 3 tablespoons (30 or 45 ml) sugar
mixed with 1 teaspoon (5 ml) cinnamon

Sift flour and salt into a bowl, make a hollow in the centre and break the egg yolks into it, put the whites in a separate bowl. Add half the milk to the flour and egg and beat well with a wooden spoon until smooth, add the rest of the milk and beat well till bubbles break the surface. Beat in the brandy. Melt the butter and add to the bowl of batter. Cover and stand in a cool place for half an hour, then fold in the stiffly beaten egg whites.

Heat enough oil in a saucepan to half cover the fritters. Peel the bananas and dip each one into the batter mixture, lower them into the hot oil and fry until golden brown and puffy, turning them over to cook evenly. Lift the fritters out with a slotted spoon and sprinkle them with the sugar and cinnamon. Serve piping hot.

COOMA PEARS
TENDER PEARS BAKED IN SWEET CITRUS JUICES

This is a most delicious and refreshing dish full of beautifully mingled fruit flavours. In the broiling Australian summers, tender pears and quenching citrus juices will restore even the most flagging appetite.

Serves 8

8 pears
4 large oranges
1 large lemon
1 tablespoon (15 ml) soft brown sugar

1 tablespoon (15 ml) honey
4 tablespoon (60 ml) granulated sugar
8 cloves

Choose pears of a uniform size that are ripe, but firm. Grate the rind from all the oranges into a small bowl. With a sharp knife carefully cut the remaining white skin and pith from two of the oranges and cut the flesh from between the segments leaving the thin membranes behind. Chop the flesh into small pieces and put them into another bowl with the brown sugar and honey.

Squeeze the juice from the remaining two oranges and the lemon and stir into the bowl containing the orange rind; stir in the granulated sugar. Core and peel the pears and set them upright in a buttered ovenproof dish that holds them compactly. Fill the pear cavities with the orange flesh mixture, pour over the sugared juices and top each pear with a whole clove. Cover with a lid or foil and bake in a moderately slow oven (170°C, 325°F, Gas 3) for 30 minutes to 1 hour. Baste the pears with the juice two or three times during the cooking time. The exact length of time will depend on the ripeness of the pears – they should feel tender when pierced with the tip of a sharp knife. Cool, and then chill thoroughly and serve with a little thin cream.

AMERICAN RECIPES FROM THE EIGHTEENTH AND NINETEENTH CENTURIES

Some of the following recipes call for cornmeal. This can be bought in Italian delicatessens, and supermarkets under the Italian name polenta.

CORN and CHICKEN CHOWDER
A SUBSTANTIAL SOUP WITH LITTLE DUMPLINGS

There are fish and shellfish chowders, vegetable and potato chowders, ham and chicken chowders. All are substantial and satisfying, a cross between a soup and a stew. This corn and chicken chowder from South Carolina uses corn kernels scraped from fresh corn cobs, but the whole kernel type of tinned sweet corn is a perfectly satisfactory substitute. The tiny dumplings are an authentic touch, but may be omitted if you are short of time.

Serves 4

1 small chicken
1 pint (568 ml) corn kernels, fresh or tinned
2 onions, sliced
7-8 sticks celery, chopped
1 bay leaf
1 blade mace
salt and freshly milled black pepper
water (see below)

For the dumplings
4 tablespoons (60 ml) plain flour
½ teaspoon (2.5 ml) baking powder
1 egg
2 tablespoons (30 ml) milk
1 oz (30 g) melted butter

Split the chicken into two halves and put them in a large saucepan with the corn kernels, onions, celery, bayleaf, mace, salt and plenty of pepper. Add enough cold water to cover the chicken, bring slowly to the boil, cover and cook gently for about 1½ hours until the chicken is very tender. Lift the chicken from the pan and allow to cool a little while you make the dumplings.

Put the flour and baking powder into a bowl. add the egg and beat well, then beat in the milk and melted butter. Allow the paste to stand while you take the chicken off the bone and cut the flesh into small pieces. Bring the pan of soup and vegetables to the boil, form the dumpling paste in tiny lumps between two small spoons and drop them into the boiling soup. When they rise to the top, add all the chicken meat and heat through thoroughly. Ladle into large soup plates and serve with fresh rolls and butter.

SHRIMP GUMBO
SHELLFISH SOUP WITH RICE, OKRA AND OTHER VEGETABLES

Gumbo is negro patois for the okra plant or its pods, several varieties of which grow in tropical and sub-tropical countries round the world. The leaves and pods of the plant contain a lot of mucilage, and it is this quality which thickens all gumbo dishes and gives them their distinctive, slightly gelatinous texture. For this recipe fresh okra is much nicer than tinned and nowadays many good greengrocers sell it. However, tinned okra, well-drained, may be used as a good substitute and is sold in delicatessens and some health food stores. This shrimp gumbo comes from Maryland and is full of southern flavours. It is soup, main course and vegetable all in one delicious steaming bowl.

Serves 4

3 tablespoons (45 ml) oil
1 lb (455 g) shrimps, peeled
2 onions, finely chopped
2 cloves garlic, crushed
1 red pepper, finely chopped
4 tomatoes
1 tablespoon (15 ml) flour
1 pint (568 ml) chicken stock

¼ pint (142 ml) white wine
salt and freshly milled black pepper
¾ lb (340 g) fresh okra or 1 14-oz (400 g) tin okra, drained and chopped into ½-in (1 cm) pieces
4 tablespoons (60 ml) cooked rice

Heat 2 tablespoons (30 ml) of the oil in a large pan; add the shrimps and toss them in the hot oil for two or three minutes. Lift the shrimps out with a slotted spoon and set aside. Add the remaining tablespoon (15 ml) of oil to the pan and fry the onion, garlic and red pepper until soft. Roughly chop the tomatoes and add them to the pan. Cook gently for a few minutes, then shake in the flour and stir thoroughly. Add the stock, wine and salt and pepper to taste and cook to thicken smoothly. Add the chopped okra to the pan, cover and cook gently for 5 minutes. Lastly add the rice and shrimps and heat through thoroughly. Serve in large soup bowls with a green salad on the side.

EGGS NEW ORLEANS
BAKED EGGS WITH CHEESE ON A BED OF VEGETABLES

A typical recipe from New Orleans, which has both Spanish and French influences in its flavour. It makes a delicious dish for a light luncheon or supper.

Serves 4

¾ lb (340 g) tomatoes
1 small green pepper
1 small onion
1 large or 2 small sticks celery
salt and freshly milled black pepper
bouquet garni (made up of 1 bay leaf, 2 sprigs thyme and 3 sprigs parsley tied in a bundle)

1 level teaspoon (5 ml) sugar
1 oz (30 g) fresh white breadcrumbs
4 eggs
2 oz (55 g) grated cheese

Scald the tomatoes and peel away the skins. Chop the tomato flesh coarsely and place in a saucepan. De-seed and chop the green pepper, peel and finely chop the onion and chop the celery. Add the vegetables to the pan along with a seasoning of salt and pepper, the bouquet garni and the sugar.

Fry the vegetables gently until sufficient juices run to prevent the vegetables sticking to the base of the pan. Cover the pan with a lid and simmer over the lowest possible heat for 15-20 minutes or until the vegetables are quite tender. Stir in the breadcrumbs and allow to cook for a further 2-3 minutes. Check the seasoning and remove the bouquet garni.

Spoon the vegetable mixture into 4 individual ramekin dishes and make a depression in the top of each one. Break an egg into each hollow and sprinkle over the grated cheese. Place in a moderate oven (180°C, 350°F, Gas 4) and bake for 10 minutes, or until the eggs have set and the cheese is melted.

TEXAS ROUND-UPS
MINCED STEAK ROLLS IN PASTRY AND GARNISHED

Served hot with grilled tomatoes or eaten cold, these Texan round-ups are delicious either way. They look attractive with the tasty filling speckled with green pepper and the pastry flecked with red pimento. It is important to buy a piece of lean steak to mince yourself, as most butcher's minced beef contains too much fat. This is a good dish for an informal party or weekend lunch with cheese and beer – it's fine for a picnic, too.

Serves 6

1 lb (455 g) lean steak
1 tablespoon (15 ml) finely chopped green pepper
1 heaped teaspoon (6.25 ml) finely chopped onion
1 level teaspoon (5 ml) salt
¼ level teaspoon (1.25 ml) freshly milled black pepper
1 teaspoon (5 ml) Worcestershire sauce
seasoned flour
butter for frying

For the pastry
8 oz (225 g) plain flour
4 level teaspoons (20 ml) baking powder
1 level teaspoon (5 ml) salt
3 oz (85 g) mixed butter and lard in equal proportions
1 tablespoon (15 ml) finely chopped tinned pimento caps
scant ¼ pint (142 ml) milk

Mince the steak and put it in a bowl with the green pepper, onion, salt, pepper and Worcestershire sauce. Handling the mixture lightly, shape into 8 small rolls and coat each one in seasoned flour. Fry in hot butter to seal and brown on all sides, then remove from the pan.

Make the pastry. Sift the flour, baking powder and salt in a mixing bowl. Rub in the mixed fats and add the drained and chopped pimento. Stir in the milk and mix with a fork to a rough dough. Turn out onto a floured surface and roll out thinly to about ¼ in (½ cm) thick. Cut into 8 equal rectangles.

Wrap each meat roll in a rectangle of pastry. Damp the edges and seal neatly. Place on a well-greased baking tin and set in a hot oven (230°C, 450°F, Gas 8) and bake for 15 minutes.

TAMALE PIE
SPICY-HOT MINCED BEEF WITH CORNMEAL AND OLIVES

A tasty layer of minced beef is spread between two layers of cornmeal mush which is then baked in the oven. The flavour has plenty of zest with the chilli powder and green pepper showing the Mexican influence on the cooking of the American Southwest.

Serves 4

1¼ pints (710 ml) water
1½ level teaspoons (7.5 ml) salt
4 oz (115 g) cornmeal
2 oz (55 g) black olives
1 medium onion

1 green pepper
4 tomatoes
2 oz (55 g) butter
1 lb (455 g) minced beef
1 level teaspoon (5 ml) chilli powder

Bring the water and 1 level teaspoon of the salt to the boil in a medium-sized saucepan. Stir in the cornmeal, mixing well to get a smooth mixture. Cover the pan and leave to cook gently over a very low heat for 30 minutes, stirring occasionally. Stone the olives and cut them into pieces. Stir them into the pan of cornmeal, remove from the heat and allow to cool a little.

Meanwhile, peel and chop the onion and de-seed and chop the green pepper. Scald the tomatoes, peel away the skins and chop the tomato flesh. Melt the butter in a large saucepan and add the onion. Cook gently for a few minutes until the onion is tender. Add the chopped green pepper and the minced beef. Stir over a fairly high heat to brown the meat. Add the tomato flesh, chilli powder, the remaining ½ teaspoon (2.5 ml) salt and remove from the heat. Spoon half the cornmeal mixture into a buttered ovenproof dish. Spread the meat mixture over, and top with a final layer of cornmeal. Dot with butter and place in the centre of a moderate oven (180°C, 350°F, Gas 4) and bake for 30 minutes.

G'SHTUPTAFUL LEW'R
BRAISED LIVER WITH SPICY STUFFING

This Pennsylvania dish has an interesting link with a very early German recipe for stuffed liver which is almost identical and was created by Max Rumpolt whose famous cookery book was published in 1604. When carved, the slices of pink liver look most attractive with alternate layers of green stuffing.

Serves 4

1 whole lamb's liver
seasoned flour
½ pint (284 ml) chicken stock
3 thin strips salted belly of pork

For the stuffing
3 oz (85 g) fresh breadcrumbs
½ small onion, finely chopped
1 heaped tablespoon (17.25 ml) chopped parsley

1 level teaspoon (5 ml) salt
½ level teaspoon (1.25 ml) freshly milled black pepper
pinch nutmeg
pinch allspice
pinch ground mace
2 tablespoons (30 ml) melted dripping
1 small egg, lightly mixed

Wash and dry the liver. Set on a board round side up and using a sharp knife cut into the liver horizontally to form a pocket which will hold the stuffing. Set aside while preparing the stuffing mixture. Put the breadcrumbs, onion, parsley, salt, pepper, nutmeg, allspice, and mace in a basin. Using a fork, stir in the melted dripping and egg. Mix to a moist but not wet consistency.

Pack the pocket in the liver with stuffing, but do not overfill it. Turn the liver flat side up and pile some more of the stuffing on to the thick end. Flap over the thin end of the liver and the two little side flaps. Secure the neat shape of the stuffed liver with string, and dredge on both sides with seasoned flour.

Put the liver in a roasting tin and add the stock – you may need more or less, according to the size of your roasting tin. The stock should come about ½in (1 cm) up the sides of the liver. Cover the liver completely with the strips of pork fat.

Set in a hot oven (230°C, 450°F, Gas 8) and cook for 15 minutes. Then reduce the heat to moderate (180°C, 350°F, Gas 4) and bake for a further 45 minutes.

When cooked remove any string and carve the liver in slices. The liquid in which the liver is cooked makes an excellent rich gravy to serve with it.

SHNITZ UND KNEPP
BOILED GAMMON WITH APPLE AND DUMPLINGS

A homely way of cooking gammon with dried apple rings and dumplings, this satisfying dish came from Pennsylvanian German settlers and is typical of their unpretentious good food.

Serves 6, with cold left over

3 lb (¼ kg) gammon, soaked overnight
3 oz (85 g) dried apple rings, soaked overnight
1 tablespoon (15 ml) demerara sugar

For the dumplings
½ lb (225 g) plain flour
½ level teaspoon (2.5 ml) baking powder
½ level teaspoon (2.5 ml) salt
¼ level teaspoon (1.25 ml) freshly milled black pepper
1 egg, lightly mixed
2 oz (55 g) melted butter
milk to mix (see below)

Put the gammon in a saucepan with fresh cold water to cover. Bring to the boil and simmer gently for 1 hour. Add the apple rings and the water in which they soaked, and the sugar. Simmer for a further 1 hour.

Meanwhile, prepare the dumplings. Sift the flour, baking powder, salt and pepper into a mixing basin. Stir in the egg, melted butter and sufficient milk to mix the ingredients to a soft dough. With floured hands, roll portions of the dough into about 10 small dumplings.

Lift the gammon and apples from the pan on to a hot serving dish and keep warm. Bring the saucepan of liquid back to the boil and gently add the dumplings. Cover and simmer for 20 minutes. When cooked, drain the dumplings from the liquor and serve with the gammon and apples.

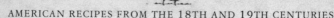

POT LIKKER WITH CORNMEAL DODGERS
HOT SOUP WITH KALE AND DUMPLINGS

If you are feeling cold and hard up there is nothing more heart-warming than this nourishing and economical dish which is full of down-to-earth country flavour. Served with bright yellow cornmeal dumplings, it conjures up a picture of the early settlers' kitchen and the women who knew how to make the best use of what simple ingredients were to hand. The old recipe used turnip tops, but as these are seldom in the shops, curly kale can be used to give an equally good flavour.

Serves 2-3

¼ lb (115 g) salt pork
2½ pints (852 ml) cold water
salt and freshly milled black pepper
1¾ lb (¼ kg) turnip tops or curly kale
(to yield about 1 lb (½ kg) greens when
picked over)

For the cornmeal dumplings
2 oz (55 g) cornmeal
½ level teaspoon (2.5 ml) salt
2 oz (55 g) plain flour
2 oz (55 g) melted butter
2-3 tablespoons (30-45 ml) cold water

Put the pork in a saucepan with the water. Bring to the boil, cover and simmer for 45 minutes. Add the greens and a seasoning of salt and pepper. Recover the pan and cook for a further 45 minutes.

About 10 minutes before the end of the cooking time prepare the dumplings. Mix the cornmeal, salt and flour in a basin. Stir in the melted butter. Add the water and mix to a dough. Mould into small dumplings with lightly floured hands – there should be enough for 12 'dodgers'.

Dish the 'pot likker' greens and the pork by tipping the liquor from the pan into a colander placed over a bowl. Lift out the pork and press the greens to remove excess liquid. Return the liquid to the saucepan and bring back to the boil. Gently drop in the cornmeal dumplings. Cover and cook for 15-20 minutes.

Meanwhile dice the pork and chop the greens. Keep hot in a warm earthenware dish. To serve, put the cooked dumplings round the edge of the dish with a good cupful of 'likker' from the pot poured over them.

JAMBALAYAH

CHICKEN PIE WITH RICE AND MIXED VEGETABLES

Rice combined with meat, fish or shellfish gives jambalayah its distinctive flavour. It is a traditional Creole dish for which there are many variations. In this case it provides a savoury way of using up cooked chicken.

Serves 4

8-12 oz (225-340 g) cooked chicken, off the bone
5 tomatoes
1 small green pepper
1 medium onion
2 sticks celery

12 oz (340 g) cooked rice
salt and pepper
stock or water (see below)
2 oz (55 g) fresh breadcrumbs
½ oz (15 g) butter

Dice the chicken flesh. Scald the tomatoes and peel away the skins. Halve and remove the seeds and then dice the tomato flesh. Seed and chop the green pepper, slice the onion and celery thinly.

Put the chicken, tomatoes, green pepper, onion, celery and cooked rice in a saucepan. Add a good seasoning of salt and pepper and pour in just enough stock or water to prevent the mixture from sticking to the base of the pan. Bring to a simmer, cover and cook gently for about 15 minutes.

Turn the mixture into a buttered pie dish. Sprinkle with the breadcrumbs and dot generously with flakes of butter. Place above centre in a hot oven (200°C, 400°F, Gas 5) and bake for 30-40 minutes, until crumbs are crisp and golden brown.

DIXIE SHORTCAKE
CORN BREAD WITH CREAMY CHICKEN FILLING

Here is an unusual way of using up some cold chicken. Diced chicken and mushrooms in a creamy sauce are sandwiched between two layers of hot corn bread and topped with more of the chicken mixture. Corn bread has a good grainy texture and is an attractive golden colour.

Serves 4

For the corn bread
3 oz (85 g) cornmeal
3 oz (85 g) plain flour
1 level teaspoon (5 ml) baking powder
½ level teaspoon (2.5 ml) salt
1 egg
6 tablespoons (90 ml) milk
1 oz (30 g) melted butter

For the chicken filling
1 lb (455 g) cooked chicken, off the bone
½ lb (225 g) mushrooms
1 oz (30 g) butter
1 heaped tablespoon (17.25 ml) plain flour
salt and freshly milled black pepper
⅓ pint (189 ml) chicken stock

Sift the cornmeal, flour, baking powder and salt in a mixing basin. Lightly mix the egg and milk and stir into the dry ingredients. Add the melted butter and mix well to make a batter. Pour into a well-greased 7-8 in (17-20 cm) square, shallow baking tin. Bake in a hot oven (220°C, 425°F, Gas 7) for 30-35 minutes.

Meanwhile, prepare the chicken filling. Remove any skin and dice the chicken flesh. Wipe and slice the mushrooms. Melt the butter in a saucepan and fry the mushrooms. Blend in the flour and then gradually add the chicken stock. Bring to the boil, stirring all the time, to thicken the sauce evenly. Season with salt and pepper, then add the diced chicken flesh and heat through gently.

Turn out the baked corn bread and when cool enough to handle, split in half lengthwise. Put one layer of corn bread in a shallow dish. Spoon over half the chicken filling. Cover with a second layer of corn bread and cut across into 4 portions. Pile the remaining chicken mixture on top and serve.

COUNTRY-STYLE DUCK
DUCK WITH VEGETABLES COOKED IN WINE

A recipe from New York State from the days when almost all of it was rural. The method would be a good way of cooking an old duck, as the long, slow simmering makes for a very tender dish, but if you are using a young bird the cooking time can be reduced a little. It keeps hot without spoiling and freezes and reheats well.

Serves 4

1 duck, 6 lb (2¾ kg)
2 tablespoons (30 ml) flour
3 tomatoes, chopped
2 leeks, washed, trimmed and thinly sliced
2 carrots, washed, trimmed and thinly sliced
6 sticks celery, washed, trimmed and thinly sliced
2 cloves garlic, peeled and crushed
½ teaspoon (2.5 ml) marjoram
½ pint (284 ml) white wine
salt and freshly milled black pepper
a small bunch of parsley

Cut the duck into six pieces (2 wings, 2 legs, 2 breasts) leaving the skin on, but trimming off any lumps of fat that are not beneath the skin. Fry the pieces in a heavy frying pan (add no extra fat) until they are brown and crisp all over. Lift the duck pieces into a large saucepan or metal casserole, sprinkle with flour and turn the pieces over. Add the tomatoes, leeks, carrots, celery, garlic and marjoram. Add the wine and salt and pepper, bring slowly to the boil, cover the pan and cook gently for 2 hours. One hour is sufficient for a very young bird.

Serve the duck in an earthenware dish, or the casserole in which it cooked; check the seasoning and sprinkle generously with chopped parsley.

SHOO-FLY PIE
PIE WITH A SWEET CRUMBLE TOPPING

This early American dish derives its picturesque name from the sweet ingredients which must have attracted swarms of flies in the old-fashioned kitchens. Molasses has a tang in spite of its sweetness and the pie remains crunchy and good whether eaten hot or cold.

Serves 6

6 oz (170 g) shortcrust pastry (page 75)
2 oz (55 g) plain flour
4 oz (115 g) brown sugar
4 oz (115 g) butter, cut in pieces

3 tablespoons molasses or black treacle
3 tablespoons (45 ml) hot water
¼ level teaspoon (1.25 ml) bicarbonate of soda

Roll out the pastry and use to line an 8-in (20-cm) pie plate. Trim the edges and set aside while preparing the crumble topping.

Sift the flour into a mixing basin and add the sugar. Add the butter cut in pieces. Rub into the mixture until evenly blended and crumbly in texture.

Stir the molasses into the hot water, add the bicarbonate of soda and stir together until it fizzes. Cool for a few moments, then pour into the pastry-lined pie plate.

Scatter the crumble mixture thickly over the molasses. Set in a moderately hot oven (180°C, 350°F, Gas 4) and bake for 35 minutes, or until the crumble is firm. Serve hot or cold with yoghurt or sour cream, which off-sets the sweetness of the pie far better than fresh cream.

BLUEBERRY PIE
PASTRY FILLED WITH DARK SWEET BLUEBERRIES

Blueberry Pie is as American and well-loved as Huckleberry Finn and, indeed, huckleberry is another name for the blueberry which abounds on high ground and in cool woods throughout the United States. This recipe comes from New England, and can be made with English bilberries (Scottish blaeberries) which are both slightly smaller than their New World counterparts, or with tinned blueberries drained from the syrup.

Serves 4

1 lb (455 g) shortcrust pastry (page 75) made with 1 lb (455 g) flour and 8 oz (225 g) fat
a little milk
1½ lb(¾ kg) blueberries

4 oz (115 g) sugar
pinch of salt
flour (see below)

Divide the pastry into two. Roll out one piece to a circle slightly larger than a 9-in (23-cm) pie plate. Allow the pastry to shrink while you butter the pie plate and remove any stalks from the blueberries. Line the plate with pastry. Fill with berries, sprinkle over the sugar and salt and lightly dredge with flour.

Roll out the remaining pastry to a circle large enough to cover the pie. Brush the pastry rim with water and cover the whole pie with the pastry top. Press round the edges to seal and trim away any excess pastry with a sharp knife. Flute the edges and cut a few slits in the top of the pie. Brush the lid with a little milk and bake in a moderately hot oven (190°C, 375°F, Gas 5) for 40-50 minutes. Serve hot or cold with a bowl of lightly whipped cream.

APPLE DOWDY
APPLES BAKED WITH LAYERS OF SWEET CRISP BREAD

A delicious pudding from Philadelphia that is like a dark and spicy Apple Charlotte. The thin slices of apple are sweetened with molasses and brown sugar and baked between two layers of crisp and sticky bread. This is a lovely pudding to warm you on a cold winter's night.

Serves 4-6

several slices of buttered bread
1½ lb (¾ kg) cooking apples
a little grated nutmeg
¼ pint (142 ml) water

2 tablespoons (30 ml) molasses or black treacle
2 tablespoons (30 ml) soft brown sugar

Butter an ovenproof dish and line the bottom and sides with the buttered slices of bread from which you have trimmed the crusts. Peel and core the apples, slice them thinly and use to fill the dish. Grate a little nutmeg over the apples and pour over the water and molasses mixed together. Sprinkle with half the sugar and top with more slices of bread, butter side up. Sprinkle over the remaining sugar and bake in a moderate oven (180°C, 350°F, Gas 4) for 1 hour. Cover with a piece of thickly buttered greaseproof paper, turn down the oven to 150°C, 300°F, Gas 2 and bake for another ¾-1 hour. Serve hot, with thin pouring cream.

A SUPERIOR BREAD PUDDING
LIGHT AS AIR BREAD PUDDING WITH EGGS AND SHERRY WINE

Thomas Jefferson, the third President of the United States, and a sportsman, musician, scholar and lawyer, had an early lifestyle that made him a connoisseur of good things. This pudding is said to be one of his favourites, and it is a very light and luscious variation of the old schoolroom version of bread-and-butter pudding. The original used apple jelly to spread over the top, but raspberry jam makes a delicious alternative.

Serves 4

2 oz (55 g) butter
1¼ pints (¾ litre) milk
4 eggs
about 4 slices stale white bread

2 fluid oz (70 ml) sherry
4 tablespoons (60 ml) sugar
apple jelly, or raspberry jam (see below)

Melt the butter in a large saucepan, add the milk and heat almost to boiling. Crack 2 of the eggs into a large bowl. Separate the remaining two eggs, setting the whites aside in a bowl and adding the yolks to the whole eggs; whisk the eggs and yolks together until light and foamy. Trim the crusts from the bread, cut into cubes and add them to the bowl of whisked eggs. Pour the slightly cooled milk mixture over the bread and add the sherry and two tablespoons (30 ml) of the sugar. Stir gently with a fork then pour into a well-buttered pie dish. Bake in a moderately hot oven (190°C, 375°F, Gas 5) for 30 minutes. Remove from the oven and spread with apple jelly or raspberry jam.

Whisk the egg whites stiffly and fold in the remaining 2 tablespoons (30 ml) sugar. Return the pudding to the oven for 5-6 minutes to set and colour the meringue. Serve hot.

WILD BLACKBERRY COBBLER
HOT BLACKBERRIES WITH A SWEET BATTER CRUST

This is a deliciously unusual way of serving blackberries in which a sweet batter crust makes a perfect topping for the rich, bubbling blackberries underneath. Serve piping hot with chilled whipped cream when the evenings are drawing in and a seasonal hot pudding is welcome. Well-drained tinned, or frozen blackberries can be substituted, but lack that special zest of the wild fruit.

Serves 4

1 lb (455 g) blackberries
6 oz (170 g) caster sugar
1 teaspoon (5 ml) lemon juice
½ oz (15 g) butter

For the topping
4 oz (115 g) plain flour
2 level teaspoons (10 ml) baking powder
½ level teaspoon (2.5 ml) salt
1 egg
2 oz (55 g) caster sugar
4 tablespoons (60 ml) milk
2 oz (55 g) melted butter

Mix the blackberries with the sugar and lemon juice and place in a 1½ pint (852 ml) pie dish. Dot with flakes of the butter and set aside while preparing the topping.

Sift the flour, baking powder and salt on to a plate. Crack the egg into a mixing basin, add the sugar and beat well to mix. Stir in the milk and the melted butter. Gradually stir in the sifted flour mixture, beating very well all the time to get a smooth batter.

Pour the batter over the berries in the pie dish and spread level. Set in the centre of a moderate oven (180°C, 350°F, Gas 4) and bake for 30-35 minutes. Serve hot with cream.

LEBKUCHEN
SPICY FRUIT CAKES WITH WALNUTS AND LEMON ICING

These spice cakes are of German origin and were probably first introduced to America through the kitchens of the Pennsylvania Dutch. The highly spiced flavour and very fruity texture of what is really more of a 'cookie' than a cake quickly became popular. Now lebkuchen are made in many American homes, particularly at Christmas. They have a soft, cake-like texture and keep well.

Makes 36

10 oz (285 g) plain flour
1 level teaspoon (5 ml) salt
1 level teaspoon (5 ml) baking powder
¼ level teaspoon (1.25 ml) ground cloves
1 level teaspoon (5 ml) ground cinnamon
1 level teaspoon (5 ml) allspice
3 large eggs
8 oz (225 g) soft brown sugar
½ lb (225 g) mixed glacé fruits such as cherries, candied peel and crystallized pineapple
4 oz (115 g) walnuts, coarsely chopped
5 tablespoons (75 ml) strong black coffee or sherry

For the icing
4 oz (115 g) sifted icing sugar
juice of ½ lemon

Sift the flour, salt, baking powder and spices on to a plate. Crack the eggs into a warm mixing basin, add the sugar and whisk until thick and light. Fold in the flour mixture, the prepared glacé fruits, the walnuts and the coffee or sherry.

Pour the batter into a large, shallow baking or roasting tin measuring approximately 14× 10 in (35× 26 cm); the batter should be about ½ in (1 cm) thick. Place above centre in a moderately hot oven (190°C, 375°F, Gas 5) and bake for 25-30 minutes.

Sieve the icing sugar into a basin and stir in enough lemon juice to make a fairly stiff paste. Spread over the lebkuchen while still warm and newly baked. Leave until cold and then cut into fingers.

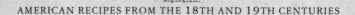

STICKY CINNAMON BUNS
SWEET YEAST BUNS WITH FRUIT AND PEEL

The Pennsylvanian settlers were famous for their home baking, and brought with them many delicious recipes like the one below.

Makes about 12 buns

1 lb (450 g) plain flour
½ level teaspoon (2.5 ml) salt
7 oz (200 g) soft brown sugar
½ pint (284 ml) mixed milk and water
1 oz (30 g) fresh yeast or 1 level
tablespoon (15 ml) dried yeast

2 oz (55 g) melted butter
4 oz (115 g) sultanas
2 oz (55 g) currants
4 oz (115 g) chopped candied peel
2 level teaspoons (10 ml) ground
cinnamon

Sift the flour and salt into a warm mixing basin. Mix in 3 tablespoons (45 ml) of sugar and set aside. Heat the liquid until a little hotter than lukewarm – about 110°F or hand-hot. Stir in 1 teaspoon (5 ml) of the sugar and sprinkle in the yeast. Set aside in a warm place for about 10 minutes or until frothy.

Pour the yeast liquid into the centre of the dry ingredients and mix to a rough dough in the basin. Turn out and knead well for 10-15 minutes to make a smooth, soft dough. Place the dough in a greased basin, cover and leave in a warm place until well risen and double in size.

Turn the risen dough on to a floured working surface and press all over with the knuckles. Roll out to about ¼ in (1 cm) thickness and brush the surface with the melted butter. Mix together the sultanas, currants, chopped peel, cinnamon and 2 oz (55 g) of the brown sugar. Sprinkle the fruit and sugar mixture over the surface of the dough. Starting at one end, roll the dough up like a Swiss roll. Cut in slices about ¾ in (3 cm) thick. Place fairly close together in a well-buttered shallow baking tin. Sprinkle with the remaining brown sugar and leave in a warm place until puffy. Set in a hot oven (220°C, 425°F, Gas 7) and bake for 20-25 minutes.

Cool on a wire tray and pull the buns apart to serve.

BIBLIOGRAPHY

Apicius, *De Re Coquinaria*
Athenaeus, *The Deipnosophists*
El Baghdadi, thirteenth century
Hannah Glasse, *The Art of Cooking made Plain and Easy,* 1760
W.A. Henderson, *Housekeeper's Instructor or Universal Family Book*, about 1805
Hunter's *Culina Famulatrix Medicinae*, 1806
Johnstone, *Cook and Housewife's Manual*, nineteenth century
F.P. de La Varenne, *The French Cook* Englished by I.D.G., 1653, third edition
Antonio Frugoli Lucchese, *Practica e Scalcaria*, 1631

John Middleton (cook to the late Duke of Bolton, 1734), *500 New Receipts*
Max Rumpolt, *Ein neu Kochbuch*, 1604

A Boke of Kokery, fifteenth century
By Several Hands, *A Collection of Above 300 Receipts in Cookery, Physick and Surgery*, 1714
Indian Domestic Economy, 1850
Leche Vyaundez, 1430
Potage Dyvers, about 1420
Southern Cook Book
The Forme of Cury, about 1390
Western Cook Book

INDEX